Ink on His Fingers

by
Louise A. Vernon

GREENLEAF PRESS
Lebanon, Tennessee

INK ON HIS FINGERS
Copyright © 1972 by Herald Press, Scottdale, PA 15683
This edition published by Greenleaf Press (Lebanon, TN 37087)
  by special arrangement with Herald Press.
ISBN 1-882514-09-2
(Previously published by Herald Press, ISBN 0-8361-1673-9)
Printed in the United States of America

10 9 8 7 6

CONTENTS

1. The Mysterious Bundle 5
2. Secret Partner 17
3. Unwilling Apprentice 25
4. Innocent or Guilty? 38
5. Surprise Discovery 48
6. Future Unknown 57
7. The Sacrifice 67
8. Man in Debt 77
9. Unspoken Threat 90
10. The Search 101
11. The Devil's Workshop 111
12. Justice by Law 120

1
The Mysterious Bundle

Shouts outside the church disturbed the final prayer of a holy day service in Mainz, Germany. Twelve-year-old Hans Dunne hurried out ahead of the others. At the bottom of the broad stone steps he discovered a lumpy bundle of coarse brown cloth with the four corners knotted on top. A boy he had never seen before was running down the deserted street and disappeared around a turn of the river road.

Hans dragged the bundle to one side. As he did so, he heard a shout.

"There he is! Stop, thief!"

Startled, Hans glanced up. Two men in leather work aprons darted from the arcade of a nearby building and ran over the rough cobblestones toward him.

"Stop, thief!"

"Stay where you are!"

The men's clenched fists and angry, red faces shocked Hans into frightened dismay. These men had mistaken him for a thief. Should he stand his ground and explain or dash back into the shelter of the church? What if the men beat him in front of the churchgoers? What would his widowed mother and his two sisters think — especially eleven-year-old Margaritte? She would tease him forever.

Hans hesitated, unable to make up his mind. Before he could reach a decision, the two men grabbed him.

"You're coming with us."

"But I didn't do anything."

The men ignored his protests, marched him back to a big house near the market square, and pushed him through a side entrance into a ground-floor shop.

"We'll see what Bertolf says about this." One of the men knocked on an inner door. A sturdy workman, with cap tilted low over his good-humored face, peered out. "Did you catch him, Lorentz?"

"Yes, Bertolf. There he is." Lorentz, small and wiry, folded his arms with an air of triumph.

Bertolf wiped ink-stained hands on his apron and came into the shop room. "But this is only a boy," he exclaimed. "What would he know about printing or typesetting?"

"What difference does that make?" Lorentz replied. "We caught him with the bundle."

"Let's see if all the types are there." Bertolf

scanned the counter and floor. "Well, where's the bundle?"

Lorentz' eyebrows shot upward as if on a string. "The bundle?" he gasped. "I guess we forgot it."

"Forgot it!" Bertolf gazed at Lorentz with a shocked expression.

"The boy didn't have the bundle on him," Lorentz explained. "It was lying on the church steps."

"Then go get it. Hurry, before master comes in."

Lorentz returned breathless. "It's gone. But it was there. I swear it."

Bertolf grunted and showed Hans a stool by the counter. "Sit down." Hans struggled, but Bertolf's short, muscular arms held him like a vise. "You stay right here. Master will decide what to do with you — as if he didn't have enough troubles plaguing him. Now look at all the time you've made us waste just to catch a thief like you."

"But I'm not —"

Bertolf's strong fingers squeezed his shoulder, and Hans subsided. His thoughts raced. Would Mother worry when she found him gone after church? No. He often went on ahead to check on old Herr Mueller's strange house guarded by watchdogs.

Why hadn't he run when he had the chance? He would be home by this time. What if these men called the constable and had him put in a dungeon? Years later, someone would find his bones and shreds of clothing. Hans lost himself in the imaginary scene. Maybe his jailers would be kind and give him paper — no, parchment — and ink, and he could fulfill his secret ambition to copy the Bible. There, on the dungeon floor, beside his bones, people would find a beautiful, illuminated Bible, just like Brother John's copy in the scriptorium at the monastery.

But in the meantime, what was going to happen to him? Did he dare lunge past the men to the freedom of the street? If he could reach the bridge without his pursuers seeing, he could hide under the arch, his favorite hiding place.

"Can't I tell my mother where I am?" he asked. "She'll worry."

"She ought to, having a little thief like you for a son."

"But I'm not a thief. I heard the shouts in church. When I came out, I saw this bundle, and I moved it so no one would trip on it."

"Maybe the boy is telling the truth," Bertolf said.

"Maybe he has an accomplice," Lorentz retorted. "The new man didn't show up today, the one Herr Fust insisted master hire. I never did trust Herr Fust. He's up to something. I told master so, but you know how he is — always trusts everyone."

"Herr Fust promised secrecy just like the rest of us, didn't he?" Bertolf asked.

"Yes, but you must remember I've been with master many more years than you. What people promise and what they do are two different things."

A slender, quick-moving man with fur-lined cap and long, parted beard hurried into the shop. His thoughtful, yet brisk, intense manner impressed Hans. This man knew what he wanted.

"Why aren't you in the workshop?" he asked the men. "We have no time to lose if we're going to keep up our quota." He glanced at Hans. "Who's this, Lorentz?"

"It's a young thief we picked up, master."

"A thief? This boy? What did he steal? Wasn't the workshop locked?"

"All we know is that a boy ran out of the shop this morning with a bundle under his arms. We figured he was stealing some types, so we chased him. He threw the bundle down on the church steps and disappeared. We hid, thinking he'd come back, and sure enough, he did. We caught him. Here he is."

"Where are the types?" the master asked.

Lorentz flushed and hung his head.

"Well?"

"The bundle was gone."

"Lorentz, Lorentz, whatever shall I do with you?" the master chided. "Now all of you get back to work. If we cast less than four thousand letters today, we'll hear about it from Herr Fust. I'll question the boy myself."

As the workmen turned toward the inner room, Hans saw his chance, sprang toward the door and out into the street. Shouts behind him spurred him on. Near the monastery he glanced over his shoulder — no one in sight. At the bridge he straddled the stone rail, hung by his hands from a jutting rock, and gained the momentum he needed to swing himself down to his favorite hiding place.

As he let go, he heard a yell from under his feet. Hans dangled by one hand and tried to claw his way up. His fingers slipped off the protruding stone knob and he dropped on top of a wriggling boy. He grabbed the other boy's wrists. To his surprise, the boy lay limp.

"Let me go. I'm not a thief."

The unexpected words, an echo of his own thoughts, astonished Hans. He jumped up so fast he cracked his head on the stone arch of the bridge. "Who are you? What are you doing? How do I know you're not a thief?" At each question Hans rubbed his head.

The boy sat up, brushed at his rumpled clothes, and straightened his battered cap. "I'm not a thief because I didn't steal anything," he retorted with spirit.

"What's your name?"

"Ulrich Zell. What's yours?"

"Hans Dunne. Why are you hiding here?"

"Because some men chased me. Why are you here?"

"For the same reason," Hans admitted. "But this is my own special hiding place."

"Why do you need one?" Ulrich asked. "Do people chase you every day?"

Hans explained. The boys who worked in the fields teased him on his way home from the monastery Latin school whenever they could catch him.

"But why?"

"Because I'm not a nobleman's son," Hans said. "They think I'm no better than they are, and that I ought to work in the fields with them instead of copying prayerbooks." Ulrich's interest almost made him forget his wild race from the shop. "Why were those men chasing you?"

"They thought I was a thief," Ulrich said. "I was looking for my uncle. He said he could get me an apprenticeship. He works for a goldsmith here in Mainz."

"A goldsmith!" Hans interrupted. "My father was

a goldsmith. He's dead, now. But go on. What happened?"

"I walked from Frankfurt early this morning — with my bundle of clothes, since I'll be living with my uncle — and went to the shop where my uncle was supposed to be —"

"Even on a holy day?" Hans exclaimed, shocked.

"Yes. Anyway, a tall, stout man was there, and I told him who I was. He let me look in the inner room to see if my uncle was there. I didn't see him. All of a sudden, these workmen started shouting 'thief' and chased me. Believe me, I ran."

"Then was that *your* bundle I found on the church steps?" Hans asked.

"Yes. Everything I own was in it. It was heavy — I had some books in it, too — so I threw it down on the church steps. I thought if the men looked at it and saw there was nothing in it except my belongings, they would leave it there and I could pick it up later."

"It's gone."

"Gone? How do you know?"

Hans explained how Lorentz, the master's servant, had run out to get it, but found nothing on the church steps.

Ulrich groaned. "But it had my own copy of the missal."

"You mean you copied it yourself?" Hans looked at Ulrich with new interest. Here was someone else who liked to copy books. "Then you've gone to Latin school."

"Of course. In Frankfurt."

"I'm going to copy the Bible someday," Hans

blurted, then choked. What had made him confide his secret dream to a stranger?

Ulrich nodded as if Hans' ambition was quite ordinary. "I've thought about that, too."

Light footsteps pattered onto the bridge.

"Hans!" a girl called.

Hans recognized his sister's voice. "It's my sister Margaritte," he whispered to Ulrich. "Don't say anything. She doesn't know about this hiding place."

"Hans, come up here. I have something to tell you."

Both boys remained silent.

"I know where you are," Margaritte called.

Exasperated, Hans waited, hoping his sister would leave. The next thing he knew, Margaritte had swung down from his very own handhold and dropped beside the two boys.

"You thought you had a secret, didn't you?" Margaritte taunted, straightening her full dark skirt. "I've known about this place for a long time." She peered at Ulrich in the shadows. "Who's your friend?"

"His name is Ulrich Zell, but you get out of here, Margaritte. This is boys' property. You don't belong. Girls aren't supposed to swing by their hands and spy on people. Go on home, and don't you dare tell anyone about this place."

Margaritte tucked a strand of hair under her tight cap and laughed. "All right, I'll go home. But you won't get to see what they're doing at Herr Muller's house."

"What is who doing?" Hans tried to suppress his excitement at the mention of Herr Mueller, their neighbor whose strange behavior had long been a mystery to the neighborhood. His three-story house, with peaked red roof, crisscross black beams, and leaded dormer windows looked like other big houses in Mainz. But why had Herr Mueller barred the ground-floor casements with iron pipes thick as a man's fingers? What did he do inside his house?

"Come on and see for yourselves, both of you," Margaritte urged.

"All right, but there'd better be something more going on than those old watchdogs barking." Hans and Ulrich helped Margaritte up the side of the bridge, and the three hurried to Herr Mueller's house.

The chimney of the mystery house belched black mushrooms of smoke. A cluster of people had gathered at a safe distance to watch. Herr Mueller's two fierce dogs lay on the front doorstep with their muzzles on their paws. At every movement they rolled their eyes without moving their heads.

"It's Satan's workshop," someone muttered.

The spectators murmured agreement.

The front door opened. A smooth-faced young man stumbled out, followed by a stout man in fur-lined cloak.

Ulrich clutched Hans' arm. "That's my uncle, and that's the man I talked to this morning."

Old man Mueller's gray hair and beard bounced with anger. He shook his fists at his unwelcome guests. "I'll pay back my loan when it is due and not a day before. Every time you come meddling and spying puts me behind in my work just that much. I don't care what Herr Gutenberg is doing or what the men in Haarlem are doing, whether I am ahead of them or behind them. Just leave me alone until the process is completed." Herr Mueller flung a brown bundle after the men. "And take your belongings with you."

Ulrich clutched Hans' arm again. "That's *my* bundle."

The stout man and Ulrich's uncle hurried away without a glance toward bundle or spectators. Herr Mueller unchained his dogs, bolted the door, and stalked off toward town.

When everyone had gone, Ulrich undid the knotted brown cloth. "This is my shirt — my books, but what's this?" He held up a leather pouch.

"Isn't it yours?" Margaritte asked.

"No. I never saw it before."

"Open it."

Ulrich opened the pouch. A handful of slender sticks fell out.

Margaritte held up a stick and ran a finger over the metal tip. "What could this be?"

Hans examined a handful. The tiny metal grooves looked somehow familiar, like letters of another language. Hans remembered something. When the monks at the monastery made wood-blocks, they had to carve the letters backward so that they would print correctly when inked and pressed face down.

With growing excitement, Hans traced one of the metal grooves again. It was an *E* molded in reverse. A glance at the other sticks showed him all the letters had been reversed, too.

All at once, Hans understood. *These were the missing types.* They had been found in the mysterious bundle — Ulrich's bundle.

"I didn't take them," Ulrich was saying.

Ulrich's astonishment sounded genuine, but an icy finger of doubt raced along Hans' spine. Was his new friend, Ulrich Zell, a thief?

2
Secret Partner

Ulrich Zell stared at the pile of types. "You believe me, don't you?"

His quiet appeal touched Hans to the quick.

"Of course we believe you, Ulrich," Margaritte said after the boys told her the story. "What an exciting mystery it all is!"

"It may be for you, Margaritte, but it won't be for either Ulrich or me if the constable finds the types in our possession. We could be put in the tower prison, you know," Hans said.

Margaritte shuddered. "I hadn't thought of that. You'll have to take the types back right away."

Hans groaned. "But don't you see? If Ulrich takes

them back, he'll be accused, and if I take them back I'll be accused."

"Then why don't *I* take them?" Margaritte asked. "I'll just explain that I found them. They wouldn't accuse a girl."

It seemed like the best solution. The boys walked with Margaritte to a corner near the shop and waited for her. When she returned, she still had the pouch.

"Nobody was there," she wailed. "I pounded and pounded on the door." She held out the leather pouch as if it were a snake. "Now what will we do? We can't just leave them."

"I'll ask the prior tomorrow when I go to school. He'll know what to do."

"I can't think of any better plan," Ulrich said. "I'm going to find my uncle and find out what he knows. I can't believe he would steal anything, and yet —" He made a gesture of helplessness.

"If you don't find him, come back and stay with us," Margaritte suggested. "Mother wouldn't mind, would she, Hans?"

"No, I'm sure she wouldn't." Hans showed Ulrich their house.

"Thank you, but if I can't find my uncle, I'll go to the monastery. The monks will take me in," Ulrich said.

Hans nodded. The monks' hospitality to wayfarers was well known.

"Besides, I'll be going to Latin school part time when I'm an apprentice. I'll see you there, Hans." With a wave, Ulrich headed for downtown Mainz.

In front of the Dunne's house, four-year-old Else ran to meet Hans and Margaritte. "Hurry! Mother says Herr Fust, the banker, is coming. We're to watch for him."

"Why would a banker come to see Mother?" Margaritte asked. "On a holy day, too."

Hans shrugged. "Who knows? Probably something about Father's estate. Anyhow, let's watch from my room."

He and the two girls raced up three flights of stairs to his favorite lookout window. Hans put the pouch of types on his sloped writing desk. He would examine them later.

"What does Herr Fust look like?" Else panted.

"How should I know?" Hans opened the casements wide and scanned the tree-lined road. "He'll have a beard, of course, and his cloak is probably lined with fur. Bankers are rich."

Else wedged herself between Hans and Margaritte. "What does a banker do?"

"He sits in his bank and waits for people to bring him their gold."

Else hitched herself up another notch. "Then was Father a banker?"

"Of course not, Else," Hans said. "Whatever gave you that idea?"

"People brought *him* gold," Else retorted.

"It wasn't the same thing at all. Father was a goldsmith." Without warning a wave of grief choked Hans. Only a short time ago Father had been alive. Then he had caught the dread fever. For the hundredth time Hans asked himself the question he could not answer. Why had God taken Father in death? What good did it to do plan ahead if a person could die almost without warning?

Else echoed his thoughts. "Why did Father die?"

"God wanted him." Hans spoke with an assurance he did not feel. "Now, stop asking questions and watch for Herr Fust."

He must be coming to talk about money. Father had been a master goldsmith. Wealthy aristocrats paid immense sums for the gold vases, candlesticks, and plates he made for them, but perhaps some of them still owed money.

Margaritte leaned over the sill. "There's a man coming."

Hans looked, too. "Margaritte, it's the same one we saw at Herr Mueller's."

They watched the stout man walk toward the house.

Margaritte clapped her hands in excitement. "Go down and let him in, Hans. Maybe you can find out something."

Hans ran downstairs and ushered the man into the drawing room.

"Are you Herr Fust, the banker?"

"Yes. You're Frau Dunne's son, I suppose."

Hans studied Herr Fust's round red face and pinched-up nostrils. The banker looked as if he smelled something unpleasant. "Yes. I'm Hans. I'll tell Mother you're here, Herr Fust."

"Please do." Herr Fust's voice trailed off.

When Mother came in, the banker coughed. "My visit here today is a matter of business. It is necessary to settle some matters about your late husband's estate." He coughed again. "I suppose young master here plans to be a goldsmith like his father?"

Mother smiled. "He hasn't decided yet. He doesn't know what he wants to be."

"I'd like to be a scribe and copy the Bible." The words tumbled out, to Hans' instant regret. Why had he revealed his secret dream for the second time that day — this time to an unpleasant man like Herr Fust?

"Do you believe you have a vocation as a scribe? You might enter the Church, perhaps?" the banker asked.

Hans thought of the many hours he had practiced with reed pen and ink shaping letters to please the exacting eye of Brother John, who trained selected scribes for the great work of copying the Bible. But to live in the monastery? Leave Mother and his sisters now that Father was gone? Hans shrank from making such an important decision.

"I'm not sure, Herr Fust."

The banker hummed, whether with satisfaction or annoyance, Hans could not tell.

"Everything will work out as God wills." Herr Fust drummed two fingers on the heavy polished table. His face was correctly grave, but his plump, twitching fingers betrayed uneasiness — and something else. Could it be greed? Hans dismissed the thought. Why would Herr Fust be greedy? He must have all the money in Mainz in his bank.

The banker cleared his throat. "I deeply regret the passing of Herr Dunne. But we cannot question God's will, can we?"

Somehow, the way he asked the question, Hans understood that Herr Fust, on the contrary, very much questioned God's will.

"It is a very painful occasion," Herr Fust began

again, and mopped his brow.

Was he trying to discuss Mother's income? Why didn't he come right out and say so? But the banker hemmed, hawed, looked out the window, put his hands behind his back, examined the frescoes and tapestries, then tugged at the ruff around his neck.

"Herr Fust, is there something on your mind — something about my husband's estate, perhaps?" Mother asked. "I'd better explain that we came back to Mainz to live because I inherited this house from my parents. Is there some problem about transferring our money?"

The banker turned squarely around. "I don't know how to tell you, Frau Dunne, but it seems your husband was in financial difficulty."

Mother gasped and pressed her hands together. "Why, how can that be? My husband had more orders than he could fill, clear up to the day he died." Her eyes filled with tears. "He always saved his money."

The banker exhaled in almost a snort. "That may have been true until recently. Of course, I know the financial history of your family here in Mainz, but —" He broke off.

"But what, Herr Fust? You must tell us."

"I never dreamed that Herr Dunne would die so suddenly and leave his affairs in such a grievous state. You see, Herr Dunne owed a large sum of money — so large, in fact, that it will take most of your income to pay for it."

Hans heard Mother's quick intake of breath. A nameless fear shot through him. Father always had strong ideas about the shamefulness of debt.

"I don't understand," Mother said over and over.

"Why would my husband go in debt?"

"Herr Dunne borrowed a large sum of money from me. I admit this surprised me, since your husband was a master goldsmith, but I am a businessman, of course. Selling money is a matter of business. I'll leave copies of the exact amount with you." He bowed. "I'll return in a day or so, and you can let me know how you plan to repay the money." He cleared his throat once more and left.

Mother sat down and pressed a hand to her forehead. "I hope it's all for the best."

"What do you mean, Mother?"

"I hadn't paid your tuition yet. The prior was very kind and said to wait until the estate was settled. Now I can't pay it. Hans, you will have to drop out of Latin school immediately."

"Oh, Mother, not now — not when —" Hans held back the torrent of words he wanted to say. Not now when he had become so sure of what he wanted to do. He held back his despair. He would have to help Mother, not hinder her.

"I didn't know you wanted to copy the Bible, Hans," Mother added. "You never told me."

"Yes, and Ulrich does, too."

"Ulrich?"

Mother listened to the whole story. "Invite him to stay here, if he does not stay with his uncle. There's plenty of room."

Suddenly, fierce ambition gnawed at Hans. Ulrich's future was all settled. But how could Hans copy the Bible if he didn't continue school? Should he become a monk and leave Mother and his sisters? Was that what God wanted him to do?

"You'll have to explain to the prior first thing tomorrow," Mother said.

That meant the prior would question him. He would have to make a decision about his future. "Mother, do you want me to become a monk, and leave you and Margaritte and Else?"

Mother's voice was steady. "If this is God's plan for you, we must make this sacrifice. We must pray for guidance and submit ourselves to His will."

Instead of submission, fiery resentment surged through Hans. Why had God awakened in him a desire to copy His Word — and then taken away the means by which he could do it? Unless, of course, he became a monk. But what would become of Mother and his sisters? Were they to become beggars like the ones he had seen on the streets with their rags, crutches, and running sores? Hans shuddered. No. He could not become a monk. *But how else could he copy the Bible?*

3
Unwilling Apprentice

Upstairs in his room Hans brooded at his desk. If only he could go on to school. . . . If only Father hadn't loaned the money. . . . If only Father hadn't died. . . .

For something to do, Hans opened the leather pouch and spread out the slender type sticks. He ran his fingertips along their grooved metal tips. On an impulse, he took a sheet of paper from his desk, dipped one finger into a squat bottle of thick red ink, and swabbed it on one of the metal tips. He pressed the metal on the paper. An *F* stood imprinted as carefully outlined as if it had been written by a scribe. Entranced, Hans printed letter after letter at random in an uneven sprawl across the page. Sometimes the ink smeared, but he managed to print several words. More and more pleased, he lost himself in the magic of instant lettering, so different from tracing each letter with a pen.

Else ran in. "Look what we found in Father's old wooden box!" She gave Hans a sheet of parchment covered with Latin words, evenly spaced across the page in black ink. Margaritte brought the box in. "There's something else in here," she said. "I can hear it rattle."

Hans pushed and pried until a thin partition gave way. While his sisters squealed in excitement, Hans lifted out two more sheets exactly like the first and several rolled up smaller sheets.

Mystified, he examined the duplicate sheets. All three had been inscribed with the same words. Hans recognized a Bible passage: "In the beginning was the Word, and the Word was with God, and the Word was God," the page began.

"It's from the Bible, isn't it?" Margaritte had made Hans teach her how to read, but she read mostly from the prayerbook.

Hans nodded, puzzled. Why would a scribe copy three pages exactly the same way? Scribes at the monastery copied page after page. Were there three different scribes at work? No. There wasn't a hair's difference on any of the words on all three sheets. Three different people couldn't write that much alike.

Baffled, Hans unrolled the other sheets. On one he found the names of Father's customers, their orders, and the price they paid. On a still smaller sheet, he found a note written in Father's painstaking writing under a date two months before he died.

> Mainz, April 8, 1452
> I have today confirmed a most remarkable miracle — God's Word in multiple, the handwriting of God Himself, yet without employing reed or stylus. In secret doth God His wonders perform, and in secret have I this day loaned the sum necessary to perfect this art. I shall not name the man, for his work must be hidden until God commands it to come forth into the full light of day.

Hans ran downstairs with the papers and spread them on the table by the kitchen fireplace. Mother examined them with a tiny frown of puzzlement.

"Hans, I've just remembered something," she said. "When your father was in his last illness, he kept talking about his secret partner. I didn't pay any attention, thinking it was the fever."

"Oh, Mother, he must have meant the loan. Don't you know anyone he might have loaned money to?" Every time he thought of the loan, hot resentment choked Hans.

She pursed her lips in thought. "I remember now that your father kept talking about some man who was doing important work for the glory of God, but I have no idea who he meant or what he meant. He kept saying this man was being blessed and inspired by God to perfect his art."

Art? What art would God inspire that took money away from people who needed it? Anger rolled up like a ball inside Hans. Father had borrowed money to lend to an unknown man. But Father had died. The man would have to pay back the loan.

"God is inspiring me, too," he thought. "Copying the Bible is important work — maybe the most important work in the world."

But how was he going to accomplish this ambition?

"I'm going to find out who Father's secret partner is," Hans announced. "I'll make him give us our money back, and then I can go back to school just as before."

The foolishness of his boast struck him at once. He could not identify the man either by name or appearance. He did not know whether the man lived in Mainz or Strasbourg. How could he even begin a search for the man who had borrowed Father's money?

He took the sheets of parchment and the note back to his room. *Who was Father's secret partner?* There must be an answer. There had to be an answer. Hans forced himself to think out the problem. Would it be one of Father's patrons? But people had to be wealthy to afford Father's skilled craftsmanship. Perhaps the man was another goldsmith. Members of the goldsmiths' guild helped each other all the time. Father would surely know the man well. Would it be a goldsmith in Strasbourg or in Mainz?

Then the answer came so quickly Hans was stunned. Who else could it be but Herr Mueller? Who else was working in secret? Who else kept himself aloof from other people? Why? Because he was working on something important.

He determined to go to Herr Mueller's, get past the watchdogs somehow, demand Father's money back. The more he thought of it, the more he was convinced Herr Mueller had borrowed the money — money which would have sent him, Hans, to school to learn the skills that would enable him to copy the Bible. He would stop first thing in the morning before he went to see the prior. Maybe he could persuade Herr Mueller to give the money back, and he would not have to drop out of school after all.

Hans slept by fits and starts that night. Without telling anyone his plans, he set out the next morning, taking the pouch of type sticks with him. He inspected Herr Mueller's house from a safe distance. Did he really have the courage to knock at the old man's door? The dogs were not outside this morning. That helped. But the tall, narrow house seemed to be waiting for something to happen.

Hans walked slower. What if he were making a foolish mistake? Would Herr Mueller set the dogs on him? Hans faltered. Perhaps it would be better to go on to school and talk to the prior first. Still, he might just knock and see what happened. But he couldn't force himself to lift his hand to the knocker.

Ashamed, he ventured a quick glance at the lower casements. With a shock, he realized someone was peering out. From inside the deep growl of the watchdogs warned him they were alert. Herr Mueller shouted something to them.

Hans started to leave. He heard the front door open and with an effort kept himself from turning around. He tried to shape his lips into a whistle, but no sound came out.

"You! You, boy!"

Hans fled. Behind him the old man's voice quivered

with anger. "Stop! Where do you think you're running off to?"

Hans whirled, heart pounding. Herr Mueller, in work apron, full sleeves pushed back, beckoned to him with an imperious gesture.

Shame burned Hans' palms. This was no way to face situations. Here he was fleeing as if he were a thief. He started back, his face hot. He had to admit to himself that he was trying to run away from something unpleasant. Glad for an excuse to approach the house, yet worried, Hans approached Herr Mueller. *Whatever happens, I won't go inside,* he told himself.

"Come closer," Herr Mueller ordered.

Hans hesitated. All the stories the neighborhood had told about the eccentric old man swarmed through his mind.

"I can't, sir."

"And why not?"

"Your dogs, sir."

"My dogs attack only at my command. If you don't come, I'll let them loose."

Hans saw the watchdogs in the narrow hallway straining at their leashes. He could not keep his gaze off their drooling, slavering jaws.

"Were you looking for me?"

"Well, yes — not exactly, sir." Hans had never been so close to Herr Mueller before. The old man's scraggly gray beard looked tangled, and his bloodshot eyes gleamed with a mixture of malice and purposefulness.

"Well, boy, are you applying for an apprenticeship?"

"Apprenticeship?" Hans faltered.

"Or perhaps you're a spy. If so, I'll have the constable take you in."

Hans stared, speechless. The very mention of the word *constable* made him wish he had left the pouch of types at home.

"Don't stand there like a country idiot. Why did you come here?"

"Please, sir, I'm here to — to — " But he couldn't get the words out. How could he ask this irritable old man to give back Father's money?

"I can't use a stupid blockhead. I need a smart boy who knows more than a smattering of Latin." A crafty, shrewd expression crossed the old man's face. "You're a spy," he announced.

"But I'm not. My name is Hans Dunne. I live up the road. I've been going to Latin school at the monastery."

"Then you must know something. You're sure he didn't send you to spy on me?"

"Why, no, sir. Who, sir?"

The old man laughed unexpectedly. "He's smart." He squinted and leaned forward. "You see he's after me."

"Who is?" In spite of himself, Hans looked over his shoulder.

The old man laughed in a derisive tone. "Oh, he's too smart than to show himself in daylight. But he knows I have the secret, and he's out to get it. He knows it will make money, and that's all he wants."

Hans shifted uneasily.

"He won't kill me. No danger of that — he just wants me to give up my secret, but that I'll never do. Now, my boy, come inside and let me hear you read

Latin for me."

To Hans, the house with its waiting dogs loomed like a monstrous prison. "I can't do that."

"You can't read Latin?" The old man asked in an incredulous voice.

"Oh, yes, I can read Latin." Sudden excitement shook Hans. His new friend Ulrich would leap at a chance to explore the house. What he could tell Ulrich when he saw him again! "I'll try."

"Follow me," Herr Mueller said.

"Yes, sir." Hans followed Herr Mueller through the dark passageway, down steep steps into a basement room. Coals gleamed from a corner fireplace, making fitful shadows on yellow walls. A long, thick worktable stood in the center of the room, with metal molds of every size piled helter-skelter on top of each other. A big bin held slivers of wood. Pungent oak balls lay clustered in one corner of the room.

"What kind of work do you do?" Hans blurted. He knew at once he should not have asked such a question.

Herr Mueller's eyes sparkled with a crafty glint. "I want a boy who will obey orders, not ask questions. My work is secret. Now, first, I want a hot, steady fire. Take those bellows."

Hans put the leather pouch of types in the corner, dropped to his knees, and pointed the long handles of the bellows toward the coals in the fireplace.

"Harder! Harder!"

The sparks shot high. The body of the flame glowed for the length of a breath, then dulled. It took a long time to get the fire hot enough for Herr Mueller's satisfaction.

"Take this." Herr Mueller thrust a long-handled pan into Hans' fingers. "Put it in the heart of the fire. Let it stay there until the metal is molten."

Moving back and forth like a crab, the old man poured hot metal in a mold, gave it a quick shake, and forced the metal into every cranny. Hundreds of tiny curves and grooves had been carved into the metal. Hans could see that these, too, were letters. Was everyone in Mainz working on this secret process? What was it to be used for? This wasn't the way block-prints were made. The monks carved out blocks of wood by hand, each block a whole page when imprinted. Why was Herr Mueller so concerned about getting metals at the right heat and, as Hans could see, mixed with the right alloys to make a proper hardness? What was he going to do with the molds?

Hans heard a knock from somewhere. Herr Mueller muttered and went upstairs. In a little while he returned talking in a loud voice. Hans peered out. A stocky man had accompanied Herr Mueller down the steep stairs, followed by two others whom Hans could not see clearly.

Herr Mueller fumed and sputtered. "You have no right to break into my house."

"As constable, I have no choice but to do my duty. Here is a search warrant signed by Johann Fust of this city," Hans heard the man say.

"But I can't pay him yet. I told him that, over and over. What does the man want — my lifeblood?" Hans Mueller moved near the workshop entrance and stood with his back to Hans.

The constable held out the warrant. "Herr Fust

claims that you are harboring stolen goods taken from the workshop of Johann Gutenberg, of this city. These goods are, namely, a hundred or so types devised and perfected by the same Johann Gutenberg, who has accompanied me."

Hans did not dare try to see what Johann Gutenberg looked like, but a suspicion began to grow. Could this be the man he had heard called *master?* Hans' heart pounded. Where could he hide the leather pouch?

Herr Mueller burst out in frenzy. "Gutenberg — Gutenberg! Everywhere I turn I hear the name Gutenberg. I know of him and his work. It's not as much of a secret as he thinks. Herr Fust told me. But Herr Gutenberg is an aristocrat. What does he have to do with a money-squeezer like Fust?"

"Never mind that," the constable said. "Now, show me over this house from top to bottom."

All at once Herr Mueller became meek. "Very well. Come upstairs."

"We'll wait here," one of the men said. Hans recognized the voice of Lorentz.

Herr Mueller grumbled and locked the workshop door. "You may be Church spies, or the king's spies, or the men from Haarlem, for all I know." Hans heard him go upstairs again, still grumbling.

Outside the workshop the two men started to talk.

"Now, Lorentz, why should he stop his experiments?"

With a thrill of alarm, Hans recognized the master's voice. So his name was Johann Gutenberg. He would remember.

Herr Gutenberg went on. "Do you think God

pours His inspirations through a trumpet into just one man's ear? No. Let him go on discovering the art for himself. He cannot harm us or what we're doing."

Lorentz made an exclamation of dismay. "But if he succeeds, all your work will be for nothing."

Herr Gutenberg laughed. "No man can prevail against God's will, Lorentz. If he succeeds, it will be God's stamp of approval."

"*Stamp* of approval. That's good. That's very good, Herr Gutenberg. You and your jokes. But what do you know about this Herr Mueller?"

"Only that he has been working almost as long as I have on the art. He's a goldsmith in good standing in the guild. Other than that, he seems to work alone."

"Master, I think Herr Fust had the new man steal our types to show Herr Mueller."

"Why would he do that? Herr Fust is my partner. Why would he lend me eight hundred gulden if he were going to betray me?"

"Oh, master, you are so trusting! Herr Fust wants someone else to perfect the art so he can buy them off and start his own printing press. If you ask me, he hid those stolen types in Herr Mueller's workshop himself. The constable will find them, put Herr Mueller in prison, and then Herr Fust can confiscate all the printing equipment, and —"

"Lorentz, Lorentz, what an imagination you have! Herr Mueller's workshop is the last place I'd look for our types."

At these words, Hans stiffened. He had put the leather pouch in the corner. What if the men came into the workshop and found them? In frantic haste, he tried to plan what he could do. Suppose he held the bundle in one hand. Then, if Herr Mueller unlocked the workshop door, Hans could run past them and out the front door. But what about the dogs? They were chained, he reminded himself.

He heard Herr Mueller and the constable return.

"And now, let us see your workshop," the constable ordered.

Hans grabbed the leather pouch and crept to the door. The moment the bolts creaked, he pushed past. Before he reached the top steps, he felt a violent tug on his legs. Hans slipped back. The bundle fell open. The type sticks lay scattered on the steps. The men picked them up.

"Here are our types, master," Lorentz exclaimed, "and here is our thief. This time he won't get away."

4

Innocent or Guilty?

Lorentz dangled a double handful of stolen types in front of Hans' nose.

"But I didn't take them," Hans began.

Johann Gutenberg lifted Hans' chin with a firm hand. "Then why did you try to run away?"

"I didn't think anyone would believe me, and when I found Ulrich, he didn't think he'd be believed either."

"Ulrich? Who's Ulrich?"

"His name is Ulrich Zell, and he's to be your apprentice — that's what he told me his uncle said."

Lorentz whistled. "That's right, master. The new lad was to come from Frankfurt — well recommended and very knowledgeable in his Latin. But why would he steal the types?"

"He didn't," Hans burst out in Ulrich's defense. "Someone put them in his bundle. He was talking to a big man in the shop, and —"

"I knew it! I knew it!" Lorentz exclaimed. "Whenever something strange happens, Herr Fust is somehow always around."

"Lorentz! Enough of that," Johann Gutenberg said. "Herr Fust is my partner."

Lorentz mumbled something inaudible but kept quiet. Hans went on with his story and noticed a look of disbelief on Lorentz' face. Too late, Hans remembered that he had not explained why he was in Herr Mueller's workshop. In despair he asked, "You believe me, don't you?" He thought of how Ulrich had made the same appeal and made a silent promise not to disbelieve anyone in the future.

He grinned in relief when Johann Gutenberg said, "Yes, I believe you. By the way, what is your name?"

"Hans Dunne."

"Hans Dunne?" Herr Gutenberg echoed. "I knew a goldsmith by that name."

"That must have been my father," Hans said. "He died in June."

Johann Gutenberg's face softened in sympathy. "So you're Hans Dunne the Younger. Your father was a fine man. He did some exacting work for me. I remember I paid him a hundred gulden." He sighed and added quickly, "He deserved every bit. But wait — that was in Strasbourg." Herr Gutenberg's eyebrows lifted in question.

"We moved to Mainz last spring — just before Father came down with the fever." Hans swallowed the familiar ache in his throat and pushed back a sudden, astonishing thought. Could Herr Gutenberg be the one Father loaned money to? But no. If Herr Gutenberg had paid Father a hundred gulden, he wouldn't turn around and borrow money from him. Besides, Herr Gutenberg was an unmistakable aristocrat. He must be rich. People like him always had income from rents and annuities.

"Coming back to the business at hand," the constable said to Gutenberg, "do you claim that these types are yours?"

"Yes."

"Are they all here?"

Gutenberg examined them. "Yes."

"In that case, gentlemen, if you are satisfied that this young man did not steal these types from you, I shall leave. I have another complaint to work on — a most peculiar charge, having to do with metal molds used by goldsmiths. It seems this peddler — who is familiar to you, I'm sure — claims that someone put some metal molds into his pack.

"Metal molds?" Herr Mueller interrupted and started to paw through the pile of metal molds on his worktable.

"Yes. Usually, these complaints are the other way around — people claim something has been stolen from them."

Herr Mueller groaned and clutched his gray hair with both hands. "I want to put in such a complaint right now," he howled. "Someone has stolen my molds — five at least. And I know who. Constable, arrest Herr Fust. He was the one."

"Herr Fust, the banker?" the constable asked, aghast. "I can't do that."

"A thief is a thief," Herr Mueller raged. "He's the only one who could have taken them. He was here. I don't trust that man."

"See, master," Lorentz said in a low voice. "I'm not the only one who doesn't trust him."

"If you have a formal complaint to make, come down to the city hall and make it," the constable said. "Gentlemen, I am beginning to wonder if every goldsmith in Mainz isn't working on this process of metal printing."

After the men left, the old man sorted out bits of metal and wood. "Now, Hans Dunne the Younger, cut this wood into strips no thicker than half your little finger, and no longer than your palm. I'm going to perfect something that will confound Herr Fust the banker thief. He can keep my molds. They will do him no good." Herr Mueller chuckled and rubbed his hands.

The exacting task tired Hans. Was there this much work to printing with letter types? He hadn't intended to become an apprentice this soon. As time passed, he became more and more desperate. How could he ever get to the monastery to see the prior about leaving school? He regretted his impulse to stop at Herr Mueller's. Why had he allowed the old man to think of him as an apprentice? What could he tell Mother? What if Herr Mueller wouldn't let him go home?

The old man fused bits of metal on the wooden strips Hans cut and arranged them into a wobbly line, face up. Hans sneaked glances as often as he dared. Herr Mueller daubed ink on the metal and pressed a piece of paper down on the type. Hans saw smudges where the ink had run, but he saw a ragged line of letters, too, just as he had done at home letter by letter. But Herr Mueller imprinted a whole line.

Herr Mueller sighed. "It just won't work."

"Let me try," Hans ventured.

Herr Mueller shrugged. Hans wiped the metal tips clean of ink. He found a brush among scraps of metal and wood that littered the worktable, dipped it into the squat bottle of ink, and traced each reversed metal letter with the same care that he used when he copied prayer missals at the monastery.

Could the Bible be copied from metal letters stamped on paper? Would it take any longer? *But the metal letters could be used again and again, and again.* . . . A strange burning understanding quivered to Hans' fingertips. He sat back absorbed in the wonder of his discovery.

Herr Mueller leaned toward him. "Put the paper over it. Quick! Before the ink dries."

Hans pressed the paper down. The letters showed up delicate and clear — but uneven.

Herr Mueller showed delight. He rubbed his hands together. "It can be done! It can be done! Ah! We will show these master craftsmen a thing or two! Now, show me how you inked those letters to make such a clean impression."

Hans took up the brush and traced a letter.

"No, no, that won't do. We must find a way that does not take so long. Otherwise, why bother using metal letters?"

An uproar from the dogs sent the old man upstairs. This time the constable and several of his men came into the workshop.

"I have a warrant for your arrest." The constable, with flush of embarrassment, unrolled a sheet of paper.

For a space of a breath, Hans thought the constable meant him. But this time, the constable addressed Herr Mueller.

"Arrest? Me? Who would do this and why?"

"You owe money to Herr Fust, do you not?"

"Yes. He knows that very well."

"You signed papers to that effect?"

"Yes, of course."

"He is now foreclosing."

Expressions of rage and bewilderment alternated on Herr Mueller's face. "But why?"

His despairing cry awakened Hans' pity.

"I am working night and day on this new process, trying to perfect it. What more can a man do? Look, I'll show you —"

The constable waved the old man aside. "I'm sorry. These are my orders, all properly signed, all within the law. My men here will take over now. Herr Fust wants everything moved out."

Herr Mueller seemed to shrivel before Hans' eyes. The constable's men began to take out everything movable.

Hans saw that he could not be of help. "I'll have to go, Herr Mueller."

The old man raised one hand in a gesture of farewell. Outside, Hans burned with indignation at the orders of Herr Fust. Why couldn't he wait for his money? Deep in thought, he almost ran into a man. Startled, he looked up and recognized the warm brown eyes and bearded face of the peddler, who did not seem to remember him.

"I thought I saw the constable go into Herr Mueller's," the peddler said.

"Yes, you did. Banker Fust is taking over Herr Mueller's workshop."

"Banker Fust is doing much mischief in Mainz with connivings and his foreclosures." As if he had said too much, the peddler hurried away.

The next morning Hans tucked the three duplicate sheets inside his shirt to show to Brother John. He arrived at the monastery early and asked the gatekeeper if he could talk to the prior. The thought of leaving school now weighed like stone on his mind. How could he have forgotten? But he had to admit that the events of the day before had made him forget. Now it loomed before him like an impassable mountain.

"The prior is in conference," the gatekeeper said. "You had better go on to class."

Hans took his place on the straw-covered floor beside his eleven classmates. Soon the monastery classroom buzzed with the drone of Latin chanted aloud. Hans' mind buzzed with all the incidents of the previous day. Was this to be his last Latin class?

The monk who taught Latin, a tall, pale man with piercing eyes, pronounced words from his prayer missal. The twelve boys repeated it. Another sentence, longer than the first hummed through the small, bare room and rebounded from the shuttered windows.

Hans mouthed the Latin words in a halfhearted attempt to respond. Where would he be this time tomorrow when he was out of school?

Hans let his imagination soar. Why couldn't he learn this mysterious new craft? Better yet, why not ask Herr Gutenberg about it? If he had to quit school, why not *become an apprentice in Herr Gutenberg's workshop*?

"Hans Dunne."

The unexpected thunder of his name jarred Hans out of his daydream. He stumbled to his feet.

"You have not joined in with your classmates for the last five sentences. Perhaps you feel that you know the church missal sufficiently and need not study further."

Hans writhed under the biting sarcasm, but swallowed his anger and shame. "*Mea culpa*," he used the customary Latin phrase to admit his guilt. What would the penance be? Helping lay brother, Reuben, in the hot kitchen — or carrying out dirty straw from the monks' cells and replacing it with fresh? But on his last day here, what difference did anything make now? Still, he would do well to keep alert. The Latin teacher often rained hearty blows on unwary students.

With an effort, Hans forced himself to recite. He had always enjoyed Latin, but not today when he knew his schooling would be over. He wished it was time for the writing class. Brother John would be interested in the parchment sheets. Perhaps the wise old scholar would advise him about the future. The thought cheered Hans so much that he outdid the others in chanting the Latin sentences. The

Latin teacher's face and bald pate glowed pink, a sign, as Hans knew from previous experience, of restrained pleasure.

The boys filed in silence down the hall to the scriptorium. Brother John did not arrive. Two monks whispered together, then led the boys back to the Latin classroom. Hans asked for permission to see the prior. On the way he heard a clatter of pots and pans in the kitchen. A shriek of protest and the sound of a scuffle aroused his curiosity. He tiptoed to the kitchen archway in time to see Reuben, the cook, tall and lank, twist about the worktable like a corkscrew.

"I've got you now." Reuben grabbed a boy by the ear. "To the prior you go."

The boy twisted and squirmed. Hans glimpsed his face. Ulrich Zell! Then his new friend must not have found his uncle, after all, and had come to the monastery. But what a way to be treated! Monks and lay brothers never showed hospitality this way. What was the matter with Reuben?

"How did you get in? Tell me that? Those walls are twice as high as a man." Reuben gave Ulrich a quick shake. "The prior will learn about you, you young thief."

Thief — *again*? Was Ulrich to be accused of being a thief wherever he went? Heavy doubt pressed on Hans. Had he been too gullible in believing Ulrich's story about the metal type sticks? Why was Ulrich being called a thief this time? There must be a reason. Hans remembered how he had defended Ulrich. Yet here he was being accused again. Was it possible for people to go through life saying one thing but doing the opposite? This time Hans refused to be taken in. He made up his mind not to trust Ulrich again.

5

Surprise Discovery

Hans did not want Ulrich to see him. He hurried down the hall and stood before the prior's closed door. Inside, men's voices rose and fell. The conference must have been going on for a long time and showed no sign of ending. Hans shifted from one foot to the other. Should he wait or should he go to his next class? Decisions, decisions. Why were there always so many? Before he could make up his mind what to do, he heard Reuben's familiar grumble, this time pitched higher than usual. Hans looked around. Reuben was propelling Ulrich ahead by holding on to his ear.

"Is the prior in there?" Reuben asked Hans.

"Yes, but someone is in there with him."

Ulrich grinned and Hans tried to smile, too, but he could not force himself to do more than grimace.

Reuben released Ulrich near the door. "I've got to see him at once. This young thief must be dealt with."

"I'm not a thief," Ulrich said, quite at ease.

Reuben glowered at him. "Why everything happens to me, I don't know. As if I didn't have enough to worry about getting up at three, busy, busy, busy all day long. And now this." He waved a flour-stained hand.

Ulrich rubbed his ear. The impish glint in his dark eyes and the way he held himself with watchful readiness aroused Hans' envy. Ulrich looked as if he didn't have a worry in the world.

Reuben continued to mourn his personal fate. "My bread's ready to come out of the oven. I can't stay here — and I can't go, not with thieves around."

"Why don't you tell him who I am, Hans?" Ulrich suggested.

After Hans explained, he saw a half-smile lurk behind Reuben's scowl.

"Just a schoolboy prank, eh?" Reuben asked. "He's going to have to talk to the prior about it, anyway. Hans, what are you doing here?"

"I have to see the prior." Hans could not bear to admit he had to leave school.

"Your friend here must see him first." Reuben cast a despairing glance toward the kitchen. "Everybody trusts you, Hans, though boys will be boys, as I know only too well. That bread has to come out of the ovens now, or the prior will put me in one of the penitent's cells down in the cellar. Horrible place. Dripping moss." Reuben shuddered. "Hans, see to it that that boy sees the prior. I have to go." He sped back to the kitchen.

Hans stiffened. What story would Ulrich have to tell this time? What if he tried to run away? With one spring he could be on his way to the front entrance and out into the courtyard. Of course the walls would stop him. Or would they?

"Ulrich, how did you get inside the monastery walls?"

Ulrich leaned against the wall. "Easy. Overhanging apple tree."

"But why did you do it that way?"

"Because some peasant boys chased me. I got away, saw the overhanging branch, and swung up on it. I was inside the walls then and didn't know what to do, so I stayed all night in one of the storehouses. The cook found me. I'll explain it all to the prior."

Hans felt better. "Explain! That's all I've been doing lately."

"Me, too."

"Ulrich, didn't you find your uncle?"

Ulrich straightened up, tense and excited. "Yes, and what a story he told! He's gone to Haarlem to be with some printers there."

"Printers?"

"Yes. You know those metal-tipped sticks? They're used in a new process for copying books. It's called printing." In his enthusiasm Ulrich looked taller and more grown up. "Johann Gutenberg has already printed a calendar — four years ago in 1448. Now he's printing his masterpiece. You'll never guess what it is."

"The Bible," Hans said promptly.

Ulrich's face fell. "How did you guess?"

Hans told all that had happened to him since he last saw Ulrich.

Ulrich pranced about in glee. "Then why don't you become an apprentice to Johann Gutenberg, too? You said you wanted to copy the Bible, didn't you?"

In a burst of insight Hans saw that God had not withheld the means by which he could copy the Bible but instead had provided an entirely new way. Even Father's death, so painfully hard to understand, had its place in God's greater plan.

The discovery thrilled Hans, but one thing puzzled him. "Why didn't your uncle stay in Mainz to help with the Bible?"

"It all goes back to the morning I came," Ulrich said. "My uncle overheard Herr Fust trying to bribe a peddler into taking that pouch of types to some patron. The peddler refused, threw the pouch down on the counter, and went out. Herr Fust sent my uncle after him, and during that time I came in. The workmen discovered the types gone, just as I looked into the workroom. *Herr Fust put that pouch into my bundle*, but he didn't want anyone to know he had them."

"But what was he trying to do?" Hans asked.

"I don't know. Anyway, my uncle said he wasn't going to spoil my chances for the apprenticeship, so he went to Haarlem."

A shuffle of sandaled feet down the hall made them both turn.

"Here comes Brother John," Hans whispered.

"I'm going to show him something. You won't run away, will you?"

"Of course not."

Brother John advanced with silent steps toward the prior's door. Hans took out the three parchment sheets from inside his shirt and spread them like a fan. "Brother John, would you look at this writing?"

Brother John's round, pleasant face turned a mottled red. "Who gave these to you? Get rid of them at once."

Hans stared in bewilderment. Had Brother John lost his senses? "Where shall I take them?" he asked.

"Any place. To the kitchen. Tell Reuben to stuff them in his fireplace."

Hans slipped past the refectory into the kitchen. Reuben, surrounded by a dozen loaves of bread, slumped over his stool half-asleep. A ladling spoon lay crisscross on the floor in a pool of cooked barley. Two mice scampered away, their whiskers prickling.

In spite of Brother John's urgency. Hans could not resist teasing the cook.

"Wake up, Reuben. The prior is coming."

"Eh, what? Oh." Reuben jumped up, looked wildly around, and pulled a heavy kettle away from the hot bricks.

Hans laughed. "I'm fooling, Reuben, but you shouldn't sleep so much."

"Up at three, to bed by eleven," Reuben grumbled. "It isn't natural." He stared at Hans. "Where is your friend? Is the prior talking to him?"

"Not yet."

"But you were supposed to watch him. I trusted you." Reuben sounded aggrieved.

"Brother John came along. He wants you to do something for him."

"Brother John has been doing a penance since day before yesterday. Ever since that banker came to talk to the prior, everyone has been upset. Brother John hasn't eaten a bite since then." Reuben narrowed his eyes in a suspicious look. "Where did you see him?"

"By the prior's cell. He's waiting to talk to him."

"He'll probably go back to the penitent's cell afterward. He needs some food. I'll fix his tray." Reuben flopped down on a wooden bench by the long worktable. "Let's see, is it bread with salt or bread without salt? I never can remember."

Hans listened to the familiar grumbling, lost in his own uneasy thoughts. Why had Brother John demanded the burning of the three sheets of parchment? They did not belong to the monastery. What had possessed Brother John to give such a command? He determined not to turn the sheets over to Reuben to be burned. Instead, he put them inside his shirt once more.

"What was the favor Brother John wanted?" Reuben stirred a kettle of barley.

"I'll be back later, Reuben," Hans answered.

On his way back to tell Ulrich, Hans spied an open door down the hall — the scriptorium, no less. Unlocked? Unheard of! Here was his chance to examine Brother John's illuminated Bible.

Hans' heart lurched with excitement and dread at the temptation. If he were caught, he would have to confess — a *mea culpa* in front of his classmates — and on top of that a heavy penance. But this was his last day. Why not take a chance? He could learn something. No one was around.

Hans beckoned Ulrich and showed him the room. "It's the scriptorium. Brother John's Bible is in there."

Ulrich's eyes widened. "But —"

"Come on. It's our only chance to see it close."

Then Hans hesitated. Enter the forbidden room? But after all, he would be copying the Bible himself someday in printing. He could compare the two ways and find out for himself the difference between printing and writing. Brother John had never let the boys within breathing distance of the precious manuscript. To touch it was unthinkable for a schoolboy. Very well, he would not touch it. But this might be the only chance they would have — ever.

The boys tiptoed inside the scriptorium. The sloped writing desks and low shelves with bound books on their sides looked different, somehow. Pale rays of sunshine filtered through the shuttered window like fingers pointing out guilt.

"Where is it?" Ulrich asked.

Hans tiptoed to a waist-high shelf at the far end of the room. The thick Bible lay on its side, longer than fingertip to elbow.

"Are you going to open it?" Ulrich whispered.

Hans hesitated. They would have to open it, after all. How else could they see what the writing was like?

The Bible, when open, made both boys gasp. The black script, in two columns, was surrounded at the margins with leafy designs colored in soft greens, blues, and reds, edged in gold.

Three unbound sheets had been tucked into the Bible. They looked familiar to Hans. As he started to examine them, he heard the shuffle of feet out in the hall. He nudged Ulrich in warning. The sheets fluttered to the floor. Hans grabbed them and to his horror saw that he had left a smudge on the parchment from his thumb, still ink-stained from his printing experiments at Herr Mueller's the day before.

Dizzy with guilt, Hans remembered his promise to himself not to touch the pages. Why had he yielded to the temptation to enter the scriptorium?

Then he realized no one had come into the room after all. He and Ulrich would not be discovered.

With trembling fingers, he picked up the sheets of parchment. *They were the same as the three sheets he had brought to show Brother John.*

"Someone copied this page three times," Ulrich exclaimed. "Is that the way they do it here?"

For answer, Hans brought out the three sheets he had brought from home and explained how he had found them in his father's box.

Ulrich grasped the truth. "Why, this is *printing*," he gasped. "But it looks just like handwriting."

The boys compared the loose pages with the same passage in the bound Bible.

The printing was perfect — not a hair's breadth of difference in the six copies.

Hans thought of his fumbling efforts to stamp metal letters on paper. Whoever had printed these six sheets was a master. But of course! Wasn't that what the workmen called Johann Gutenberg?

Hans lost himself in a daydream. He and Ulrich would be the first apprentices in the great art of printing.

"We'd better leave," Ulrich whispered. "Put the

pages back."

Hans heard a half-whisper in the hall. He had presence of mind enough to cram the three smudged parchment sheets inside his shirt and insert the three clean ones into the Bible. Too late! Someone was coming in.

6
Future Unknown

Hans faced the door burning under the slow shame of his disobedience. Why had he allowed himself to carry out the forbidden act of examining the priceless Bible? Ulrich's tenseness showed him his friend was just as ashamed. Hans braced himself. Who was coming in? What would the penance be?

Reuben stuck his head around the door. "I saw you boys come in here. I was wondering what you were up to, but I knew I could trust you, Hans."

Hans covered up a fresh surge of shame with a grin. "Why did you scare us like that, Reuben?"

"Aren't you boys always playing tricks on me?" Reuben demanded. "But you'd better come out of there. I think the prior is coming this way with a visitor."

Hans choked with fresh panic. "What will we do?"

Reuben grinned. "I have a big pail of water and two brushes out here. I think if you boys were found down on your knees scrubbing the floor for dear life, the prior would think it was a penance for some mischief in the classroom."

Hans and Ulrich bounded to the door, grabbed the brushes, and flung themselves on their knees.

"Thank you, Reuben," Hans whispered, with head ducked down. Ulrich echoed the thanks. Both boys scrubbed the floor with such pent-up zeal that Reuben chuckled. "I think this penance will do you both good." He left, humming an odd little tune.

The prior and his visitor approached. The prior paused. Hans looked no higher than his sandaled feet. He could see the visitor's pointed shoes of fine leather once, but much worn. Then he heard a voice he recognized. "No, I assure you, I did not authorize such sample pages to be brought here. Who gave them to Brother John?" Johann Gutenberg demanded.

"I do not know. Brother John would not say, and he voluntarily undertook a penance for disobedience."

Using the scrub brushes, Hans and Ulrich moved away on all fours. What if Johann Gutenberg discovered them and found out about their disobedience? What a fine introduction that would be for two would-be apprentices!

"Brother John tells me the loose pages are in the Bible, here in the scriptorium." The prior took Johann Gutenberg inside but did not shut the door.

Hans and Ulrich glanced at each other and scrubbed their way back to the doorway.

"Are these from your printing press, Herr Gutenberg?" Hans heard the prior ask.

"Yes, but I can't understand how they got here. I had made a number of these trial pages to show to a few people, and I brought some to show you."

"For what reason?"

"To borrow the money I need to continue printing the Bible."

"But Herr Gutenberg, I understand from other sources that you are in debt — deeply in debt."

"That is true. I have lived in debt or on the edge of debt for many years. I could not worry about money matters when I was working so hard to perfect my printing press.

"Now, Herr Gutenberg, just when do you expect to pay back your debts? Next year?"

"Impossible!"

"The year after?"

Johann Gutenberg sounded desperate. "You must understand it will take years to print even a hundred copies of the Bible. If it were not for friends, I would have had to give up before this."

On hands and knees at the doorway, Hans listened in stunned disbelief. Now everything was clear. *Johann Gutenberg must be the man who had Father's money.*

The prior persisted in his questioning. "But you cannot guarantee either payments or Bibles, can you?"

"My presses work day and night, but who can guarantee the future? Only God knows."

Down the hall, Hans' classmates droned the multiplication tables. Hans shuddered with dislike and moved his scrubbing brush with forceful strokes. Columns of figures baffled him. At least one thing was sure. He would never have to earn a living using mathematics.

"Now, Herr Gutenberg, do you claim that God has divinely inspired you?" the prior asked.

"I claim nothing," Herr Gutenberg replied in a spirited voice. "Whatever gifts God has given me, they are designed for His greater glory. This new art will mark a new era in spreading God's Word."

"But if this new art, as you call it, takes hold, what will become of our scribes? Their skills have been cultivated for centuries. Are we to send them all to till the fields?"

"Of course not," Johann Gutenberg replied. "They will use the same skills in a different way. They will no longer have to waste their talent copying grammar books for schoolboys. Instead, they will disseminate the Word of God by teaching people to read His Word."

"This is dreamer's prattle. We cannot improve upon perfection. It is true that a scribe puts in many days, months, even years, to copy a book by hand, but that is God's way. If He wanted it done differently, He would have ordained it from the beginning."

"Do you mean there are no new revelations?"

"Herr Gutenberg," the prior responded, "let us not enter into a purposeless discussion. I do not want any more samples of your so-called art in this monastery. We cannot lend you money on such a venture as this. You might go bankrupt. We cannot take the risk."

Hans heard the prior's verdict with a sinking heart. Would Gutenberg have to quit printing the Bible? Hans felt a wave of dedication rise up within him. He understood why Father gave so willingly. There must be a way that he and Ulrich could help. Never mind about Father's loan. Who else was undertaking such an exciting work?

"I'm going to talk to the prior as soon as Herr Gutenberg leaves," he whispered to Ulrich.

The sound of his own name jerked Hans to startled attention.

"Hans Dunne! What do you want with him?" the prior asked.

"I knew his father in Strasbourg. I have reason to believe the boy is brilliant. Isn't he of an age to be an apprentice?"

Hans strained to listen. Never mind feeling guilty about eavesdropping now. He had better listen. His future was at stake. Elation filled him. He would be Johann Gutenberg's apprentice. This was God's plan for him. There could be no doubt of that now.

"What about me?" Ulrich whispered.

"You're already his apprentice — as soon as you show up. Lorentz said they were expecting you," Hans whispered back. "You could be starting in right now if you were there. Why don't you go talk to Brother John? Ask Reuben. He knows where the penitents' cells are."

Ulrich nodded and left.

The prior and Johann Gutenberg came out into the hall.

"May I talk to Hans Dunne before I leave?" Gutenberg asked.

Hans held his breath for the answer.

"I am afraid I must refuse. His father's recent death has been a great shock to the boy. He needs time to adjust. He is brilliant, as you say, but it would not be wise to plunge him into worldly interest."

"Do you call reproducing the Bible in multiple a worldly interest?"

"You must excuse me, Herr Gutenberg. I must return to my other duties. I bid you Godspeed, Herr Gutenberg," the prior said, "but I insist that you keep your devilish so-called art out of this monastery. I have had enough of it."

Soon after Gutenberg left, Hans faced the prior who stood by his highbacked walnut chair carved with the story of David and Jonathan. The prior asked the question Hans had been dreading.

"Now, Hans, what are you going to do with your life?"

Hans' courage failed. "I just haven't been able to decide."

Somehow, he just could not explain his hope to be an apprentice to Johann Gutenberg.

The prior fingered a white cord around his long brown robe. "It is high time that a twelve-year-old boy make up his mind, especially under the circumstances."

Hans twitched with surprise. Had he misheard the prior's earlier statement to Johann Gutenberg — that he should not be hurried into a decision?

"God has granted you many gifts, Hans."

"Yes, sir."

"He often bestows great gifts on the weak and unworthy."

Hans nodded.

"Do you not think it right to give your life to God in return?"

"My life?" Hans echoed.

"For every gift, God demands a sacrifice, Hans."

"But how could I use my gifts if I gave up my life?"

The prior smiled. "That is just a way of speaking. I mean that you would give up the world and enter the Church."

"Would I become a scribe?" Hans asked.

"You will become whatever God wills."

"Would I have to live here in the monastery?" Hans looked at the prior's heavy brown habit. How could a person move around in one of those?

"Of course you would live here. Your studies will continue. God's plan for you will gradually unfold to the extent that you seek to know His will. Of course, you will have to face many temptations."

Hans winced.

"Overcoming them will make you stronger. Now, Hans, I feel your place in life is right here in the monastery. The Church needs you. Will you come to her?"

Hans twisted under the prior's forthright appeal. "Is there any way I could go on to Latin school the way I have been?"

"Yes. We will take you as a charity student until you are of age to enter the monastery as a novice." The prior rose and stood under the high barred window with his hands behind his back.

Hans took a deep breath. How could he agree? Why hadn't he told the prior that he wanted to be Gutenberg's apprentice?

"I must in all fairness tell you that a businessman has offered you an apprenticeship."

Hans' hopes soared.

"Yes, Herr Fust tells me you are intelligent, and he is willing to take you as apprentice in his bank."

Banker Fust again! Hans disliked him more than ever. Was he trying to make up for taking so much of Mother's income?

Hans groaned. "You mean I'd work with figures all day long — adding and subtracting?"

"Mathematics is not your strongest subject," the prior admitted, with a hint of a smile. "But you are free to choose your own future, Hans. Pray about this, my boy. You may be sure that God will listen to earnest pleas. He has a plan for each of us, if we will only subject our pride to His will. Perhaps with His help you have already arrived at a decision."

Hans shook his head in despair. What should he do? Decide! Decide! A sea of uncertainty engulfed him.

"I don't want to be an apprentice to Herr Fust," he told the prior. His firm statement surprised and pleased him. Maybe making decisions wasn't so hard, after all.

The prior smiled. "The choice is yours. I presume, then, that you have decided to enter the Church."

At once a hot denial sprang to Hans' lips. "No — I didn't mean that." Could he shut himself up within the walls of a monastery forever? Was this the way

God meant him to achieve his goal of copying the Bible, after all? Was Johann Gutenberg, with his printing art, just a temptation to try him?

The white walls of the prior's cell pressed in on Hans. He had to break out of the tiny, stifling room. What was the choice? Banker Fust? Never. The Church? How could he? But did he dare risk becoming an apprentice for a man as deep in debt as Johann Gutenberg?

7
The Sacrifice

Hans jumped up. "I can't give you my answer now," he told the prior.

"Suppose you talk to Brother John," the prior said.

"Oh, may I?"

"Yes, of course. He has often told me how talented you are."

"But he wasn't in the classroom today," Hans faltered. Should he admit he knew where Brother John was?

"No. He has undergone a voluntary penance, but you may go see him. Do you understand the true nature of a penance, Hans?"

"Yes." Hans felt sure about that point. A penance

meant punishment for wrongdoing.

The prior smiled. "Perhaps you will learn something more from Brother John."

What could the prior mean? Hans thought about his remark on the way to the kitchen. What did the prior want him to understand? Was it connected somehow with the decision he had to make about his future?

Hans found Ulrich talking to Reuben. "Brother John wants to talk to us together," he said, "so I waited. Do you remember the footsteps we heard the first time and no one came in? That was Brother John. He saw us."

Then why hadn't he come in? Hans wondered.

Reuben gave Hans a tray. "Take this tray to Brother John, will you?" Reuben asked. "Third cell to the right in the cellar."

The tray held a container of water and a tiny loaf of bread.

"Is this all he gets to eat?" Hans' stomach became hollow at the thought. Would he be half-starved if he entered the monastery?

"Maybe it's all right to give him another." Reuben plopped another loaf on the tray.

As Hans started out, the prior appeared in the doorway. "Who is this boy?"

"His name is Ulrich Zell, and he wants to talk to you, and Brother John wants to talk to us both, and —"

The prior cut him short. "Very well. Ulrich, you see me afterward. Now, what are you doing with this tray?"

"Taking it to Brother John."

"Why are there two loaves of bread here?" The prior sounded stern.

"Oh, Your Excellency," Reuben sputtered, "the loaves were so small — hardly more than a mouthful each — and Brother John hasn't eaten since night before last. I thought —"

"It is not your duty to think but to obey. Those who give themselves to God must learn obedience first of all. Remove one of these loaves."

"Of course. At once." Reuben snatched off a miniature loaf and laid it on the stone oven. Only a tiny loaf of bread, a tankard of water, and a pinch of salt remained.

"That is better," the prior said. "Now Hans, you may go. Perhaps you will learn something today about the spirit of sacrifice and obedience."

Hans and Ulrich started down the winding stone steps to the cellar. Footsteps pattered behind them. Reuben, with a wild glance around, put two more loaves of bread on the tray.

At first Hans grinned. Then he hesitated. Should he take the extra bread back, remove it himself, or leave it on the tray? Decisions, again! "Brother John will know what to do," Ulrich said.

Brother John's cell of cold damp stone contained only straw, a basin, a stool, and table.

Hans introduced Ulrich in some embarrassment. Would Brother John start questioning them right away about being in the scriptorium? But Brother John appeared in no hurry to say anything.

Hans and Ulrich watched him eat one loaf of bread and take a sip of water.

"Brother John, why do you have to be punished

like this?" Hans blurted.

Brother John looked up. "I'm not being punished. I'm doing penance."

"But why do they force this on you?"

"It wasn't forced. I chose this of my own free will."

"To live in a prison?" Hans could not see why Brother John would want to live in isolation like this — Brother John, the great scholar, who in a spirit of sacrifice corrected schoolboy mistakes and whose serene cheerfulness was like sunshine.

"I am happy to isolate myself for a time. Here I follow the path of purification. My body is confined, true, but my spirit is free. By mortifying my body, I purify my love of Christ. Do you think I look unhappy?"

Hans studied Brother John's serene face. "No. You look very happy. But you can't do your work down here. You will lose so much time."

"Time is the gift of God," Brother John replied, "and obedience to His will is the gift of man."

"Then what is a sacrifice?" Hans asked.

Brother John smiled. "You will have to discover that for yourselves. What is a sacrifice for one may not be a sacrifice for another."

After this remark silence hung heavy in the little cell. Hans' guilt pressed in on him. He looked at Ulrich and burst out, "Ulrich is going to be an apprentice to Johann Gutenberg." The whole story gushed out. "And I want to be his apprentice, too," Hans finished.

"But I thought you wanted to become a scribe. Have you abandoned the idea of copying the Bible?"

"No, Brother John. Don't you see? This way it will

be in printing — like those parchment sheets in the scriptorium." There. His guilty secret was out.

Brother John did not seem to hear the mention of the scriptorium. "Printing?" he asked. "What is printing?"

"Writing with metal letters." Hans explained what he knew about the process. "The metal letters are lined up, daubed with ink — like wood-blocking, only the letters can be taken out and used over and over."

Brother John paced the floor, his face alight with interest. "Printing! Of course! That's the answer to the puzzle. But why didn't Herr Fust say so, instead of letting me think those sheets were hand-copied. I had never seen such perfect handwriting, I told him." Brother John stopped. An expression of awe crossed his face. "The man who did this is a genius — a God-inspired genius."

"Then why does God make it so hard for him?" Hans asked. "He's in debt, and maybe he won't get to finish printing the Bible."

"Ah!" Brother John said. "The sacrifice. God never makes His way easy. He tests us by opposites." With this puzzling remark, he dismissed the boys.

When Ulrich went to talk to the prior, it was agreed that Ulrich should stay at the Dunnes' house until the boys' future had been settled. Hans left Ulrich with the prior and started home to notify his mother of Ulrich's coming.

Outside the monastery walls, the trees lining the river never seemed greener nor the water bluer. Hans reveled in the feeling of freedom.

Ahead, at the bridge, a group of peasant boys

waited. Rusty, the red-haired, stocky boy, leader, as usual, waited ahead of the others.

Hans advanced with caution. Rusty met him.

"If it isn't old Inky Fingers himself. What are you doing on my territory?"

"I want to cross the bridge." Hans spoke in a level voice. He secretly enjoyed the encounters with the cocky peasant boy.

Rusty planted his feet apart. "This is a toll bridge." He held out his hand. "Two groschen, please."

Hans ignored the request. "Let me by."

" 'Let me by.' 'Let me by,' " Rusty mocked. "Who do you think you are? We're just as good as you, even if we don't go to Latin school. How much ink did you get on your fingers today? Open your hands."

"I won't." Hans put them behind his back.

"We'll make you." Rusty signaled. Three or four boys sprang to his side. Rusty grabbed at Hans' fingers.

The fight began. The boys pushed, ducked, and punched. Three boys threw Hans down. Someone's knee pressed his stomach. Another boy's foot pinioned his leg. Rusty forced Hans' fingers open.

"Not as much as usual," he reported, "but why don't we wash his hands for him?"

"Yes, yes," the other boys chimed. "Throw him in the river."

The boys on Hans scrambled to their feet. As Hans sprang up, his shirt loosened. The three parchment sheets fell out.

Rusty held the sheets upside down between middle finger and thumb. "What's that black stuff?" A curious note of defiance and yearning in his voice touched Hans' sympathy. *Why, he wants to know,* he thought. Was that why Rusty had teased him so much before? Was he really hungry for knowledge?

"That's writing. Look, I'll show you." Hans bent down and traced big letters in the dirt. "There. Those are the letters of your name — *Rusty.* You do it."

Rusty traced his name. "Is that really my name? You're not fooling?"

Hans showed Rusty the tiny black marks on the parchment. "These are letters, too."

"But they all look the same."

While Rusty held the parchment, Hans pointed out the words and read the passage: "In the beginning was the Word. . . ."

One of the other peasant boys, impatient, grabbed the parchment and ran. With a yell, Rusty ran after him.

Another boy called a warning. "Someone's coming."

The someone turned out to be Herr Fust, who glanced at the parchment Rusty had grabbed from his teasing friend. The next thing Hans knew, Herr Fust had seized Rusty by the jerkin and was shaking him. "Where did you get these, you little thief? I'll have you flogged."

Too startled to move, Rusty only stared up at the big man. A sudden powerful rage mixed with the newborn sympathy he felt for Rusty welled up in Hans. He was not going to stand by and let Rusty be blamed for something not his fault.

He ran up to the scowling man. "Those are my father's papers, Herr Fust. The ones you took from Herr Gutenberg are at the monastery."

Herr Fust released Rusty and strode off. Rusty lingered near Hans with a grin of gratitude.

Then Hans had an inspiration. "Listen, Rusty, go to the monastery and ask to be a charity student. They'll teach you all you want to know."

Rusty ran off with another grin, but Hans knew he had understood.

Hans went home, well satisfied. Ulrich came soon after. Mother made him welcome and the whole family listened to the story of the day's events. Hans did not mention his conviction that Johann Gutenberg was the one Father had loaned the money to. Mother would never believe it.

As they sat down to supper, Else began to whimper, "I'm afraid."

"Afraid of what," Hans asked.

"The dogs. They're barking."

"They can't hurt you. Herr Mueller keeps them tied up all the time.

Margaritte listened. "They're loose. They're coming this way."

Hans bolted the door. The barking came closer and louder.

A loud thump on the door startled them.

"Quick! Let me in," a man panted. "The dogs will tear me to pieces."

Hans unbolted the door. The peddler stumbled into the house, bent under his huge pack. Hans slammed the door shut. Outside the dogs bayed in disappointment.

"Why, it's the peddler," Mother said.

A loud knock interrupted her. Herr Mueller came in, apologizing for his dogs. "Thought you were Herr

Fust," he told the peddler. "I've warned him and warned him to stay away from my house, but he never listens. I mistook you for him. Please accept my apologies."

The peddler nodded, and Herr Mueller left.

"Sit down by the fireplace," Mother urged the peddler, "and tell us the news."

"Thank you, thank you." Over his rust-colored beard, the peddler's earnest brown eyes widened in surprise. "Why, Frau Dunne, I didn't recognize you at first. I thought you were living in Strasbourg."

"We came here to the house my parents left," Mother explained. "My husband died here this year."

The peddler murmured his sympathy. "Herr Dunne was a fine goldsmith. I suppose your son here will become a goldsmith, too?"

"He and his friend, Ulrich, plan to be apprentices to Herr Gutenberg —"

A strange expression crossed the peddler's face. Instead of the open, sympathetic gaze of a few moments before, the peddler with lowered eyelids fumbled at his pack. "I feel I should warn you. Herr Gutenberg is a goldsmith, but his is a strange craft, not of God, as he hopes, but of Satan."

"But how can that possibly be?"

"I can't say more — I dare not say more. It is not Herr Gutenberg's doing. He is hardworking and honest in intent, but I warn you, do not let these boys become apprentices there."

The peddler slung his pack over his shoulder and hurried away. He had hardly gone before another knock sounded. Hans opened the door. Herr Gutenberg stood in the doorway with eyes burning and his face pale.

Inside, he stammered, "I just found out — my partner, Herr Fust, told me — it was your husband who loaned me a great sum of money when I needed it. I need much money for my work, but I have always borrowed from people who could afford it. I would never in the world involve a family's welfare and future, and since your husband is dead — Frau Dunne, I had no idea who the patron was until today when my partner told me. I'm here to return the money to you."

Now Hans understood what a sacrifice meant. *If Johann Gutenberg repaid the debt at this time, he would not be able to go on printing the Bible.*

8
Man in Debt

Johann Gutenberg held out a money pouch. Hans recalled with painful intensity his vow to make the man who had borrowed Father's money return it all. Here it was — but now he did not want the money, and he knew Mother would not want it either. The printing of the Bible must come first.

Mother spoke Hans' thoughts. "We know about your great work, Herr Gutenberg. We wouldn't dream of taking back the money when you need it most." She gently pushed the pouch back.

Hans sensed Gutenberg's relief.

"It's a big sacrifice to ask of you and your children," Gutenberg said, "but I assure you when the

Bible is printed and sold, you will not only receive your money back but will share in the profits."

Hans and Ulrich exchanged glances. Now was the time to ask about the apprenticeships. Hans waited for Ulrich to speak first. After all, he was already registered as an apprentice, but he would have to explain his delay in arrival.

Margaritte broke the spell. "Herr Gutenberg, this is Ulrich Zell. He's your apprentice, and my brother wants to be an apprentice, too."

A burst of excited questions and answers followed. Within the next few days, through the pope's approval of his plans, Gutenberg won the prior's approval, too. Soon, arrangements had been made for the two boys to finish their schooling at the monastery's Latin school while being part-time apprentices. Ulrich began his apprenticeship first. Hans had to wait until 1454.

When the day finally came for him to start work at Johann Gutenberg's printing shop, Hans woke early. Had the night really passed this fast? He had slept only a little while, he was sure, yet he could see light. The sun was up. What was he doing in bed? He swung his legs to the floor, his heart pounding with excitement and anticipation.

This was the day he had been waiting for, his mother had waited for, and his two sisters had waited for. Everyone had talked of this day when Hans would start his apprenticeship.

Hans took a deep breath. The next he knew, sunlight flooded the room through the tiny dormer window. He bounded up, his heart in his throat. What had happened? Why hadn't Mother called him? He listened. There was no sound upstairs or downstairs. He put on loose green trousers, a white shirt with full sleeves, and a brown, sleeveless jerkin. He looked into his sisters' room. The bed, already made up, looked as if no one had slept there. Panicky, Hans tiptoed downstairs. Mother and his two sisters sat at the table with heads bowed. Hans waited until Mother said "amen" and slipped onto his bench without a sound.

Mother smiled. "We didn't wake you, Hans — not this morning. There is plenty of time."

"Are you going to be an appwentice?" Else whispered, wide-eyed, when Hans had finished breakfast. She tugged at his jerkin. "Are you going to be an appwentice?" she repeated.

"You mean apprentice." Hans made Else pronounce the r.

"I can say it," Margaritte announced with a toss of her head. "Apprentice, apprentice, apprentice," she chanted.

Tears welled in little Else's eyes. "Is that what you're going to be?"

Amused, yet touched by Else's concern, Hans grinned down at her. "You don't even know what it is, so what makes you think it's bad?" He hugged his mother and sisters and started off.

"What *is* an apprentice?" Else wailed after him.

"Ask Mother," Hans said over his shoulder. He tried to smile, but his lips felt parched. Leaving was harder than he thought it would be. This morning marked a new way of life. Already the familiar countryside, with its slopes of grass and trees looked unfamiliar. Dark shadows burrowed into hollows he had never noticed before. The tips of his toes stung with cold. He threw back his shoulders and resisted the impulse to look back. He might as well get used to the new life right now.

In a little while he turned into the street near Johann Gutenberg's hidden workshop.

An old market woman dressed in a dirty, russet-colored gown, plucked him by the sleeve. "Be ye the young master who is going to work for —" She rolled her eyes in the direction of the printshop. "Herr Gutenberg?"

"Why, yes," Hans stammered. How did this old woman know something like that when no one else knew as yet?

She laughed with eyes closed, her red tongue pressed against snags of teeth. Putting her finger to her lips she hunched over and whispered. "I have old eyes, but nothing escapes them. I am here first in the morning and last at night. What I don't see, I overhear. What I don't overhear, I see." She threw back her head and cackled. Her clawlike fingers dug into Hans' arm. "Think twice, young master, think twice."

"Why? What is the matter with working for Herr Gutenberg? People have apprentices, and that's what I'll be, just like other boys my age."

She moved her head in slow disagreement. "You are stepping into a fearsome tunnel without end. This man is not an ordinary man —"

"I know that," Hans interrupted. "He is a great man. Someday everyone in the whole world will know his name."

"Herr Gutenberg is in league with Satan." The old

woman put her hand over her sunken mouth. Her eyes gleamed with vitality and malice.

Hans stammered, "What do you mean?"

"Tell me this — has he not made you promise strictest secrecy?"

Hans was flustered. How could the secret which he was so sure no one knew be on the lips of an old crone like this? And come to think of it, why was Herr Gutenberg so secretive? Wasn't his business a legal one? *Was* he doing something wrong?

The old crone cackled again. "Not only that, has he not promised you great glory for the work you will be doing?"

Discomfited, Hans had to admit Johann Gutenberg had made such a promise.

"Has he not apologized for lack of money and sworn that he would share with everyone who helped? They who are taken in by false prophets will suffer eternal torments," the old woman hissed. "You must listen for the truth. You must not let greed step in."

"But it is not greed — I don't think it is." Hans pulled away. Why had he chosen apprenticeship with this man — of noble birth, it was true — who had such struggles? Why didn't God help if Gutenberg was doing His work? To be as deeply in debt as Gutenberg was not the way of God or man.

Hans shifted his weight on the rough cobblestones. Should he go into the shop or shouldn't he?

The old woman watched him with glittering eyes and a half smile. "Think twice, young master. Do not enter Satan's workshop."

With a sudden spurt of determination, Hans grabbed her withered arm. "How do you know all this?"

She shrank back. "I have my messengers."

"Yes, but who. Tell me." He gave her a shake and she trembled like a dry leaf in the wind.

"Now, don't be so upset, young master. Every morning a rich man comes by my stall and buys an apple —"

"Is he a tall man — heavy-set?"

She nodded.

Hans let go of her arm. Relief flooded him. Herr Fust again. Was he poisoning all of Mainz against Johann Gutenberg?

With firm decision, Hans entered Gutenberg's printing shop. Ulrich met him. "I'll show you around. Everybody is busy, so don't talk. There's something else, too." Ulrich lowered his voice. "Herr Fust insisted that the master hire a new man for a few weeks. His name is Peter Schoeffer, and he's going on to Paris afterward. But there's something strange about it all. Anyway, come inside."

Ulrich opened the door to the inner workshop, a room crowded with men who worked around a huge, heavy-beamed press. Hans recognized Bertolf, who stirred something in a huge, round copper tub. Another sat before a sloped case.

Daylight filtered through double windows of yellow disks framed in black. The light from the windows, the red glow in the fireplace, the subdued voices of the men, and the crunch of the heavy press excited Hans in a way he had never felt before.

Ulrich explained Hans' first duties. "You have to keep the floor clean — and keep out of everybody's way. I have to keep the fire going." Ulrich went to the six-cornered fireplace and began to work the

bellows in the square firehole.

Hans spent the day picking up scraps of metal and slivers of wood, mopping up daubs of ink and water, and listening to the crunch of the heavy press. For each printed page, a man had to twist the sturdy handle to lower the press so that the bed of metal type impressed the parchment sheets.

In the late afternoon while Gutenberg was out, a quarrel broke out between Peter Schoeffer, the man Herr Fust had hired, and Lorentz, Gutenberg's worker.

"I do not like the way you refer to our master," Lorentz said.

"And I do not like the way your master takes credit for something that you know nothing about," Peter Schoeffer retorted.

"Why don't you go on to Paris, if that's where you're going?" Lorentz taunted.

"Paris is a better place than Mainz. But I shall stay until I have proof that your master is nothing but a common thief."

Lorentz shook his fist under Peter's nose. "Say that once again in the presence of these witnesses, and Herr Fust will have to carry you out. It is a pity that honest men who have invented something useful should be so maligned."

"Your Herr Gutenberg did not invent movable type. Laurent de Coster of Haarlem invented it before you were even born."

"That is not true," Lorentz retorted. "My master has told me all about movable type. The Chinese knew it centuries ago. My master said the minute someone carved a letter and pressed it on a woodcut, it was movable type. But I won't argue with you about that. I say that my master, Johann Gutenberg, took all these bits and scraps of ideas and put them together and made it into an art."

"And I say he copied, stole, and sneaked it away from Laurent de Coster of Haarlem."

With these words, the two men flung themselves on each other with fists pounding. Hans watched, fascinated. Ulrich ran out and returned with the master.

The stern voice of Johann Gutenberg interrupted the fighters. "Stop! Both of you! Do you want to ruin my life's work? Lorentz, I'm ashamed of you."

Lorentz lowered his fists. Peter Schoeffer dabbed at a bleeding nose. The next day Peter Schoeffer left for Paris. The printing of the Bible went on. Hans and Ulrich worked, watched, and listened. Johann Gutenberg busied himself with more experiments, sometimes casting even smaller metal letters, and sometimes working on metal molds for the large, initial letters.

One day Lorentz hurried to the desk by the window where Johann Gutenberg sat engraving a tiny piece of metal. Hans, broom in hand, listened.

"Master, there are some city councilmen outside. They say you will have to join the carpenters' guild."

Gutenberg half rose from his chair. "Why, Lorentz, that is ridiculous. I am already affiliated with the goldsmiths' guild. What more do they want?"

The city councilmen burst into the workshop. Gutenberg sprang from his chair. "Gentlemen, this is a private workshop," he thundered.

"Herr Gutenberg, you will have to answer some

questions," a councilman said. "In your work, do you not cut out letters of wood?"

"Not any more. The ink softens wood too much."

One of the councilmen picked up a handful of slender, metal-tipped sticks from the sloped letter case. "See? These have wooden stems. That is all we need to know."

The leader nodded. "There is a petition of wheelwrights, carpenters, turners, and coopers demanding that you join their guild."

Gutenberg flung his hands up. "Go tell this carpenters' guild that I will not join. Lorentz, show this man out."

Later, Lorentz brought back the news that the carpenters were meeting at their guildhouse to vote on whether Johann Gutenberg should join.

Gutenberg sent Lorentz and Hans to the guildhouse to report on the vote. Hans was to run back as soon as the vote had been decided.

Outside the guildhouse men discussed the matter.

"This man Gutenberg should be run out of Mainz again — just like his father was twenty years ago," one of the carpenters said.

"They weren't run out — it was voluntary exile. You know very well the patricians never could get along with the guilds."

"Well, I never heard of a patrician joining a goldsmiths' guild."

"But what other guild could he belong to?" a spokesman for the goldsmiths asked. "He works with metals. He carves in metal, and pours hot metal into molds. That is all done in our craft."

"I tell you, this man Gutenberg, for all his high

birth, is not an honorable man," another said.

"Why so? You'd better be careful — he'll have you before the city council," someone else warned.

"I know for a fact that when he was in Strasbourg, he had several lawsuits on his hands. Can such a man be honorable? Most of the lawsuits had to do with money. Why does this man always borrow money? What does he do with it all?"

"An artist cannot be a practical businessman," a guildsman observed.

"But if he is impractical, who is to look after him?"

"He is doing God's work."

The head of the carpenters' guild called out, "We must settle this one way or another. How many say that Johann Gutenberg should join the carpenters' guild?"

The vote was *no*. Hans raced back to tell Gutenberg the news. Gutenberg grunted with satisfaction and turned back to his metal carving.

A few days later in the workshop, before the workmen came in for the day, Hans was picking up shavings from the floor. He heard Lorentz talking to Gutenberg.

"Master, I do not wish to disturb you," Lorentz said, "but the bill collectors are here."

"Bill collectors?"

"Yes. They say they must have payment."

"What for?"

"The paper you ordered last June."

"Ask them to wait for a few more weeks. We're well under way with the Bible. Surely they understand that we can't stop now."

87

"They said you said that the last three times."

Gutenberg sighed. "But I haven't any money."

"Sir, have you forgotten your annuity?"

"Bless you, so I had — but that's not until January 6 — Epiphany. Tell them to come back and I'll give it all to them."

"All? Twenty gulden? But, master —"

"Now, Lorentz, why must you wrangle over everything? Yes, we'll pay it all to them."

"But master, what I was going to say was, aren't you forgetting your other bills?"

"Haven't we paid them?"

Lorentz sighed in his turn. "Neither for the ink, nor the tools, the metals — to say nothing of the men's wages and the rent. Add the parchment and the paper to this and —"

Hans heard Gutenberg stand up and pace between the press and the fireplace. "Stop, Lorentz. I remember only too well, but what can I do? Why can't people have faith? I do. God will provide."

An angry roar of voices sounded outside. The door burst open and several men pushed their way in waving rolled-up papers.

"Herr Gutenberg, we have come to collect the money you owe us," one said.

Gutenberg pointed to the press. "Your money lies there if you will only have patience, gentlemen."

"We want our money now. We have waited long enough."

"I have no money."

"How long before this so-called great work of yours will be finished?"

"Another three years," Gutenberg said.

The bill collectors roared in dismay. "Three years? We can't wait. We'll have the law stop this printing nonsense of yours. Go back to goldsmithing and earn the money to pay your debts."

When the men left, Gutenberg sat down at his desk, head in his hands.

Once again doubts tormented Hans. *Why would God permit the printing of the Bible to be stopped?* It was a question he could not answer.

9

Unspoken Threat

The threat from the bill collectors did not stop Johann Gutenberg from continuing to print the Bible. Every day the skilled workers arrived, set up type, wielded the heavy press, and dried the damp sheets of parchment. Hans and Ulrich kept the floors clean and the fire going. Every day Lorentz admitted Herr Fust, the banker, into the printing shop. Herr Fust, big and bustling, probed, questioned, and complained about the expenses.

"Why does he have to stick his nose in everything?" the workmen grumbled to each other. "Master wanted the art to be kept secret."

Lorentz hushed them. "Master needs another loan."

Herr Fust fussed and fumed, but made the loan to Gutenberg.

"Eight hundred florins, same as last time," the word went around the shop. "Herr Fust is a full partner. Master had to sign away the whole shop as security."

This news stunned the workmen.

"He wouldn't sign it away unless he knew we'd finish the Bible soon," someone volunteered. "And then we'll all make money. I heard of a man who made a thousand gulden one year just from the sale of manuscripts. Think of the money our Bible will bring in."

Gutenberg, always in a careful hurry, said little, but his eyes gleamed when the printed sheets were lifted one by one in a steady procession from the press, ready to be dried and folded.

Months passed. At home Margaritte had taught Else how to read. At the monastery, Rusty, the peasant boy, had proved to be a quick learner. He, too, had ink-stained fingers from learning to write, but he grinned in good humor when Hans and Ulrich teased him.

In 1454 Herr Fust brought back Peter Schoeffer. "Here is your new foreman," he told Gutenberg. "He has studied in Paris, and he is skilled."

Behind Herr Fust's back the workers grumbled about the new foreman. He soon proved himself a master of the printing art. He could set type faster than anyone else, but no one liked him.

One day Gutenberg summoned Hans and Ulrich. "The Bible will soon be finished. We'll have to make plans for the future." He winced and hunched his shoulders, as if trying to shrug off something unpleasant. "The time will come when I will no longer be here, but the art of printing must not die. New printers must be trained. Do you boys intend to take up printing as your lifework?"

"Yes," they chorused.

"Then it is time to start your training."

He led them over to where Peter Schoeffer sat at the compositor's desk, a slanted board raised on crisscross stilts. "Peter, I want you to train these boys, one at a time, in setting up types."

Peter looked annoyed. "There is no time for that," he snapped.

But Gutenberg insisted with a strange urgency. When Hans' turn came, he stood by the slanted case with a feeling of excitement and dread. Peter Schoeffer's gruffness had already become the talk of the printing shop. His long beard, sullen mouth, and drooping eyelids seemed to shut out sounds, smells, and even people. Hans did not dare speak.

At last Peter growled an acknowledgment of Hans' presence. "What do you want?"

Hans stammered something.

"Speak into my left ear, boy. Don't mumble."

"I think Herr Gutenberg wants you to teach me."

"You think! Don't you know?"

Peter's surly question aroused Hans' indignation. "Sir, the master wants me to learn to set type."

Peter grunted. "All right. Watch me and tell me what you see."

Hans stared at the case. He noticed first that there were pockets of every size crammed with metal-tipped sticks. Peter's hand flashed back and forth from pocket to pocket. He slid the metal letters into a grooved board he held in his left hand.

"Well?" Peter asked. "What do you see in the case?"

"Different-shaped pockets all crammed full of letters."

"Are the letters in alphabetical order?"

Hans studied the pockets. "No. Here's E in the biggest pocket."

"Why is that?" Peter asked.

At first Hans could think of no reason at all. "Because there are more Es in words than other letters?"

"Right. Now read the line I have in my stick," Peter ordered.

Hans studied it. "I can't. It's all backward."

"Then you are going to have to learn to read backward, aren't you?"

The half-sneer in Peter's voice aroused Hans' determination to master typesetting. He leaned on the case to study the other letters.

"Stand erect," Peter snapped. "Face the case. Don't lean. Find each letter, one by one, pick it out of its slot, handle it, look at it, and put it back. You can practice when no one else is here, but don't mix the types."

In this way Hans began to learn the craft of printing.

In the days that followed, Hans practiced every chance he could. He discovered the letters most used were in the middle of the case, easily reached. Smaller slots at the side of the case held the least-used letters.

Sure of himself at last, he approached Peter. "I

know where the letters are," he said.

Peter tested him without comment. Hans felt rebuffed. Hadn't he learned this lesson well enough to suit Peter?

Peter grunted approval, and even smiled a little. Hans' spirit soared. That was more like it. He knew he had done well.

"Now put this blindfold on." Peter produced a long cloth.

Hans wrapped it around his eyes, puzzled.

"Now, hand me the letters that I call."

Hans gasped. He reached, fumbled, and dropped letters.

"When you know your letters, let me know," Peter said with a derisive chuckle.

Later Hans overheard Peter Schoeffer talking to Herr Fust.

"You shouldn't have let him use only forty-two lines." Peter insisted.

"How could I prevent it?" Herr Fust asked.

"Couldn't you see that he could have squeezed?"

Herr Fust looked puzzled.

Peter sounded impatient. "Squeezed more lines onto a page. He could easily have put forty-eight lines instead of forty-two."

"How?" Herr Fust asked.

"By filing off the upper and lower sides of the metal and leaving less white space between each line. When we set up our printing shop, that's what we'll do."

Hans gasped. Had he heard right? Would Herr Fust and Peter Schoeffer set up their own shop? Was that why Herr Fust had been so inquisitive? He ran to tell Lorentz in the front shop. Lorentz sat on a bench, hands tucked into his sleeves, looking glumly at the floor.

"Did you know about Peter and Herr Fust?" Hans blurted.

"You mean about the rival printing shop they are going to set up?" Lorentz did not even look up.

"Doesn't the master know?"

Lorentz shook his head.

"Aren't you going to tell him?"

Again Lorentz shook his head. "It would do no good. He won't listen to anything but what has to do with the Bible. He's eating and sleeping the Bible until it's done. The money is running low again. This time, Herr Fust will foreclose and master will lose everything — everything he's worked for all his life."

"But God will help him," Hans stammered.

"God isn't man-made law," Lorentz said. "Master has had lawsuits before. Why can't people understand that he's an artist? Why can't they let him alone? Why should he have to worry about money all the time?"

Hans could not answer these questions. His thoughts had raced ahead. "Do you think Herr Fust and Peter will start their shop before the Bible is finished?"

"That's what is worrying me," Lorentz replied.

A little later, Hans saw a man lingering outside the shop. He walked with tense movements back and forth. The man seemed to have a stiff neck. When he turned, his whole body turned with his head. Hans noted the sturdy build, the coarse, red face, and wide, tight mouth.

With a last look around, the man patted something under his cloak, and stepped into the narrow doorway. He blinked at the interior darkness, and his breath came in hoarse gasps.

"Anyone here?" the man asked in a deep tremulous voice.

Hans kept in the shadows. Somehow, he did not trust the man.

The unwanted visitor called again, then took out a sheaf of papers, laid them on the counter, and slapped his open palm against the polished wood. Hans stepped out into the shop.

The man looked at him with disdain. "Is your father here?"

"No." Hans stared at the papers. They had a legal look.

"Find him, then. I have important business with him."

"It isn't my father."

The man drummed the counter with impatient fingers. "The person I want to see is Johann Gutenberg."

Lorentz came out of the inner workshop, saw the man, and whirled to go, but the man caught him. "Not so fast. Where is Herr Gutenberg?"

"How do I know?" Lorentz answered in a spirited voice. "He has other business than tending shop here. He is a patrician."

"Patrician or not, he can get into debt just like common people," the visitor snapped.

"Herr Gutenberg comes from an old and distinguished family that has lived in Mainz for centuries.

His father was one of four master accountants here in Mainz, and his uncle was master of the episcopal mint. Herr Gutenberg himself —"

The man broke in. "I don't care about all that. I want to see your master, not talk about him."

"Herr Gutenberg is an honest man," Lorentz said.

"Then let him own up to his debts and pay them. Where is he?"

"He is at work on something very important — not just for himself but for all of Germany — maybe the whole world."

"Then why doesn't he finish it and make money to pay off debts that are twelve years old?" the man asked.

Lorentz paled. "Twelve-year-old debts? But he returned to Mainz only in 1448, six years ago."

"Before that, did he not live in Strasbourg?"

Lorentz sank back on the bench visibly shaken.

A sound made Hans turn. Gutenberg came into the front shop, head down, hands behind his back, lost, Hans could see, in that realm of the imagination where inspiration dwells.

"Herr Gutenberg?" the visitor asked.

"Yes. What is it?" Gutenberg's tired, forced smile pained Hans' heart.

"I have come for the interest you owe."

Gutenberg put a hand to his forehead. "Interest?"

"Yes, yes. I have copies of documents here from Strasbourg. Now Herr Gutenberg, isn't it true that in 1442 you and Martin Brechter appeared before an ecclesiastical judge in Strasbourg and drew up an agreement to obtain a loan of eighty pounds from the St. Thomas Chapter?"

"Yes, it is true."

"And is it not true that you agreed to pay 5 percent interest, using as security an annuity of ten florins a year settled on you by your late granduncle, Johann Leheymer, and payable by the city of Mainz?"

"Yes, yes. Lorentz, pay him the interest." Gutenberg handed his money pouch to Lorentz, who reluctantly paid the man.

"And now, please excuse me," Gutenberg said.

The man did not go. "There is another matter, too. Did you not obtain a loan of one hundred and fifty gulden in 1448 from a relative of yours, one Arnold Gelthuss?"

Gutenberg groaned. "Yes. It is on the city records. But surely he understands what a gigantic task I have undertaken. He will get his money back. With God's help, everyone will." He sighed. "Please go. I must go on with my work."

The man hesitated, fingered the money Gutenberg had given him, and left.

On the way home in the late afternoon, Hans and Ulrich talked over the day's events. Near old man Mueller's house, Hans saw Herr Mueller himself pacing in front.

"I was looking for you boys," he called to them. "Come inside to the workshop. I have something important to tell you."

Hans and Ulrich exchanged glances. The old man had become more of a recluse than ever since Herr Fust had taken away his equipment. To their surprise, the old man's workshop looked almost the same as before. "Don't tell anyone," the old man whispered. "I'm still experimenting, thanks to Herr Gutenberg. He shared his tools with me. He knows what kind of man Herr Fust is, though he's never said anything, but he knows, he knows." The old man lowered his voice, "That's what I want to talk to you about. Herr Fust is setting up his own printing shop. Go tell Herr Gutenberg at once."

"We heard this rumor, too," Hans said. "But nothing has come of it."

"He is setting it up right now," the old man insisted. "Tomorrow is a holy day. You keep watch, and see if I'm not right. Workmen are going to move one of the heavy presses to Herr Fust's house."

Somehow the old man's words rang true. The next day Hans, Ulrich, Margaritte, and Else took turns watching. Else made the discovery. "Here they come," she shouted.

The others hurried to the third floor lookout window. Several men in workmen's clothes of short, full trousers, full-sleeved shirts, and sleeveless jerkins pushed a two-wheeled cart loaded with heavy beams. At each step the men grunted with strain. Their shoulder-length hair flopped about their faces. The men stopped to rest.

"I say Herr Fust should move his own winepress," a worker complained.

"This press distills a secret wine," another retorted.

The men roared with laughter. Another man caught up with the workmen and called out, "Hurry up. There is no time to waste. Herr Fust is waiting."

Hans recognized Peter Schoeffer. The realization hit him and Ulrich at the same time. Peter Schoeffer, the foreman of Gutenberg's press, had just revealed himself as a traitor.

10
The Search

By the time Hans and Ulrich reached the printing shop the next day, all the workers had heard the bad news. Johann Gutenberg had been handed a summons by Herr Fust's lawyers, demanding his appearance at court for nonpayment of debts.

"Master," Lorentz implored, "give me leave to find a patron for you who will pay off all your debts."

"It doesn't matter now. The Bible is almost finished," Gutenberg told him.

Almost finished — almost finished. The words echoed through the shop. The binding and rubricating were to be done by Heinrich Cremer, vicar of St. Stephen's, a skilled craftsman. When the first copy was assembled, Gutenberg gathered all the workmen together in the printing shop, placed the big book on a table. He opened it at the Gospel of St. Luke. Once more Hans saw double column of black script, like Brother John's handwritten copy of the Bible in the scriptorium.

The initial letter, a bulging square with gold, blue, and red tracings showed delicate whorls like tiny veins of trees with buds at their junctures. The design at the bottom showed leaf curled on leaf, extending from a curved stem in blue, maroon, pale green, pink, with pale dots of gold underneath in a fragile fretwork.

When everyone had satisfied himself looking at the Bible, Gutenberg raised both hands. "Let us pray," he said. All knelt. "O God, our Father, Thou hast blessed this workroom of Thy servants. May we understand and practice all that we have printed here. Let us continue to work according to Thy law, and not for reward, lest our labor be without blessing and bring evil on our souls. May all that we have done and will do be for love of Thee, and in Thy holy name. Amen."

Afterward, a worker complained about the way the Bible was set up. "The master could have got six to ten more lines to a page if he hadn't allowed all that fancywork. Would have saved paper and parchment. He wouldn't have gone into debt. Him and his patrician ways. Only the best he'd have, though he had to borrow money from everywhere."

Hans knew without being told that this workman would go to Herr Fust's and Peter Schoeffer's printing shop. Who else would leave Gutenberg? After all, Herr Fust could afford to pay well. Was there a patron in Mainz who would help Gutenberg?

Lorentz drew Hans aside. "Your father was a master goldsmith, wasn't he?"

"Yes."

"He knew most of the rich people here in Mainz, didn't he?"

"I suppose so. He had many orders for his work."

"Didn't he keep a list of names someplace?"

"I suppose he must have. Why?"

"Don't you see — if you could get those names, we could ask them one by one to be a patron. Will you bring me a list of his customers?"

Hans found the record of his father's Mainz customers in the wooden box at home. By each name he found the order that had been made, the date it was finished, and the price paid. To Hans' amazement, the payment column for a number of people had been left blank. Hadn't they paid, then?

In excitement, he brought the list to Lorentz. "We'll go to these first," Lorentz bobbed his head in glee. "Maybe we won't even have to have a patron. This will just be payment of old debts." He selected several of Gutenberg's printed calendars to show people.

At the first house they stopped at the woman explained that her husband had gone on a trip to Italy to buy books. "What is it you wanted?"

Hans explained who he was, and the debt her husband owed for the goldsmith work.

"Oh, your father made this vase." She pointed to an intricately carved vase on a table. "It's beautiful, isn't it? I wish I could pay you, but I have only enough money for housekeeping. Come back in three weeks. My husband should be here by then. I can't imagine why he hadn't paid this before."

"Three weeks! That will be too late for us. Master will be in court by then," Lorentz groaned.

At the next house a servant ushered Hans and Lorentz into a large room with carved bookcases on three sides. The metal clasps of embossed books gleamed from the shelves. On a long, low table, scrolls and bound books of handwritten script lay open. This patron must be a scholar, Hans thought.

The patron himself appeared at the doorway. There was no mistaking the patrician tilt of his head, the well-groomed silky beard, the smooth, graceful movements, the subtle richness of his clothes. Hans felt the patron's penetrating stare. He stood without quivering under the flick of the man's slightly contemptuous gaze.

"I understand you have a manuscript you wish to show me?"

Lorentz held out a printed calendar printed by Gutenberg in 1448.

"What is this — a joke?" The patron scanned the calendar. "It is a beautiful handwriting, of course, but I am a collector of books, not parchment sheets."

"This is the new process called printing," Hans explained.

"Printing?"

"Yes, writing with metal." Hans launched into an explanation, but the patron cut him short.

"Just what are you trying to sell me?"

"If you will lend Herr Gutenberg the money he needs to pay his debts, you will have your investment back as soon as the Bibles are finished and sold."

The patron waved both hands in an effort to stem Hans' words. "Stop! I have the finest collection of manuscripts in my private library between here and Cologne — maybe further. My books are all one of a kind. Do you think I would patronize copies of books — even the Bible — *in multiple*? Every copy the same? Never."

He waved them out of the house, as if brushing dirt off his hands.

The next name on the list was that of a lawyer whose office was in the front room of his house. He sat at his desk, listened to Hans' explanation, and shook his head.

"I'm afraid a mechanical device like this printing press you describe will be only temporary. It will never take the place of handwriting. Oh, I do not doubt Herr Gutenberg's sincerity. He comes from a fine old family. But I'm afraid this scheme of his is harebrained. A work written on parchment will last a thousand years. A volume on paper — how long? A hundred, two hundred at the most."

"But many of the Bibles are on parchment," Hans explained. "They were printed on both parchment and paper."

But the lawyer dismissed Hans and Lorentz with a shake of his head. On the street, they studied the list again.

"Why not try a bookseller? I understand there is a bookstall by the church."

"But booksellers live by the skin of their teeth," Lorentz objected.

"Not this one. He has money salted away, I am sure."

At the bookstall, the bookseller listened with bright-eyed interest. Then he shook his head.

"What makes you think many men will buy these printed books?"

"Because already they save their money to buy woodcuts of St. Christopher — even the poorest saves up money for that."

"But of course," the bookseller said. "That is understandable. Doesn't St. Christopher protect us all from accidents? It is only natural that a man's eyes rest upon St. Christopher the minute he wakes up in the morning." He added, "I have one myself, dated 1423."

"Well, then, won't people save money to buy copies of God's own Word?"

Two women turned down by the church from the marketplace. "Food is far too dear," one was saying. "What are prices coming to? We can't even keep body and soul alive. But I couldn't see three groschen for a cheese. I'll go without, first."

Then she saw the block pictures in the bookstall. "Oh, isn't that St. Christopher?" she asked the bookseller. He came instantly to her side. "Yes, the patron saint of all who work. But you undoubtedly do not have to work, madam."

Hans could see that the flattery disarmed the woman. It was as if the bookseller assumed she was a fine lady.

"I-I work," she admitted.

"Then it would be well for you to — in fact, necessary, if you wish to be kept safe during the day — to open your eyes upon the face of St. Christopher the minute you wake up in the morning. Then you will have a saint's blessing near you all day long."

"But I'm sure I cannot afford the price. How much is it?"

"Three groschen." The bookseller looked at her sharply. "That is the price for ordinary buyers, but I could let you have it for two and a half groschen."

The two women whispered. The first one shook her head but kept looking at the woodcut. "I must buy cheeses to eat. There is a long winter ahead."

"But what if you or your husband took ill — what then? This picture will protect you. Why, I know three women who warded off death by having this picture. Perhaps you know the burgomeister's wife?"

The woman's eyes widened with astonishment.

"Yes, the burgomeister's wife, no less. If she hadn't had that picture by her bed, her husband would have been a dead man. Only three weeks ago, it was."

The woman reached into a purse dangling from her waist. "Very well, I'll take it. Two and a half groschen, you say?"

"And a half more for the gilt around the frame," the bookseller said smoothly. "Look at that face. Doesn't it seem as if it smiled at you? These artists are skilled with their wood-carving these days. Nothing will take the place of their skill," he added.

The woman handed over the money, took the picture in both hands, kissed it, and turned away talking excitedly to her companion.

The bookseller turned back to Hans and Lorentz. "I cannot promise the help you need. You see my poor establishment here. I am only a poor entrepreneur, a seller of books, yes, but only for an exclusive clientele. My scribes write only on order. So you see I am circumscribed. More books — less pay. Would you have my scribes, who've spent their lives at writing, starve?"

"But you have truncated passages, omitted texts, added paragraphs. Herr Gutenberg's invention means perfect copies — each one like the other. Think what this will mean in the future — a Bible in the hands of every person on earth." Lorentz no longer sounded like a servant.

"Is that Herr Gutenberg's intention — to have everyone have Bibles?"

"He foresees this in the distant future, yes."

"But not everyone knows Latin. How will they learn?"

"People like the Brothers of the Common Life will teach people. But that is not Herr Gutenberg's concern at this time. He needs money to pay his debts. Will you help?" Lorentz pleaded.

But the bookseller refused.

"Not enough call for books," he concluded.

A man ran up. "Can you tell me where I can get a copy of the homilies of Haimon?"

"It depends on how much you're willing to give for it."

"I don't have money, but I'll give you a hundred sheep."

"That isn't enough."

"I'll throw in five measures of wheat."

The bookseller considered. "But the homilies are like truth in gold."

"Well, I'll add five measures of barley, and if that isn't enough, I won't be able to have the book." The man sighed, and started to turn away.

"Very well. It cuts down on my profit, but I can see you're a lover of books." The bookseller told the man where to take the sheep and grain. "Then come here for your copy."

"Thank you, thank you. I will cherish this book above all else."

The bookseller avoided Lorentz' and Hans' eyes and bustled about his stall dusting off his wood-blocks.

They consulted their list again. Time was short.

"Perhaps if we could persuade a rich man to come and see the actual press and the printed sheets, he would be impressed," Hans suggested.

Lorentz at first objected. "You know how master wants to keep the printing art a secret. He made us all take an oath."

"But what good will a promise to keep it secret be if he loses everything?"

They persuaded a cloth dealer to come with them to the shop. When Hans opened the inner door to the workshop, the visitor gasped. Hans could see that the huge press, the octagonal fireplace, and the sheets of paper strung out to dry baffled the man.

"What! Did you want to show me a winepress?"

"Sweeter wine comes from that press than any you have ever tasted," Lorentz said. "See these?" He pointed to the printed sheets.

The cloth dealer stared at them. "But it is marvelous. Why, I see the work here of a thousand hands bearing pens. Do you mean to say that handwriting can now be duplicated?"

"Yes. But master is in debt. He needs money to pay for printing the Bible."

"What will the scribes in the monastery do? Are they to give up a thousand-year tradition? Does the Church approve?"

Lorentz answered the last question first. "The pope approves. He sees that printing is for the glory of God."

"May I see how printing is done?"

Lorentz nodded.

"More ink!" a pressman called. Another workman dabbed two round, wool-padded skins covered with ink on the type bed. Another workman placed paper on the bed. The pressman pulled at the bar that lowered the screw and pressed the paper onto the type. When the press was released, the workman lifted the damp paper with its black imprint.

"It's marvelous, incredible, a miracle," the cloth dealer breathed.

"Then you'll lend the money to Herr Gutenberg?" Lorentz asked.

The cloth dealer sighed. "I'm afraid not. You see, I owe a big sum of money to Herr Fust, the banker. I borrowed it to buy cloth. Of course I'll get my money back and more too, but right now, I have hardly enough to live on. I am very sorry." He left the shop expressing more regret.

Hans sighed and looked at his list. "Conrad Homery, Syndic," he read. "What's a syndic?"

"Some kind of city officer," Lorentz told him. "But it's no use going on. We'll just have to let Herr Fust have his lawsuit."

Sick at heart, Hans could only agree.

11
The Devil's Workshop

For many days Hans sensed the undercurrent of tension in Gutenberg's printing shop.

"Gutenberg will lose the lawsuit, and then where will we be?" some of the workmen asked.

"Herr Fust and Peter Schoeffer are setting up a printshop of their own. We'd better go there. The money is sure," one man said.

Another gave his opinion. "This newfangled business won't last, no matter how much money there is. Look how long it has taken to turn out one hundred Bibles — five years."

Bertolf von Hanau, a workman always loyal to Gutenberg, defended printing. "How long would it take to have a hundred Bibles handwritten?"

The disgruntled workman had an answer. "The people who can read want their books handwritten, the way God meant for them to be. Printing will put all the writing monks out of work."

"I agree," another workman said. "This printing will never take hold. I say back to the old-fashioned way — fingers clenched around an honest quill and applied to a bit of parchment, or vellum — or, I grant you, this paper. I can see where the paper business might last."

Bertolf spoke up. "The time will come when there will be a printers' guild, just like goldsmiths, or carpenters, or saddlemakers, or any craftsmen."

The workers hooted in derision.

Heinrich Keifer, another loyal worker, added, "Even so, this man Fust is sneaky. He never works in the open. I never did trust him."

The workmen murmured agreement.

Hans sensed the tide had turned. Now the workers who had disparaged printing stood up for their master. Again the remarks flowed.

"Yes, he pays up fair and square when he does have the money."

"It makes a man wonder if the hand of God isn't somewhere in this. The Church has given its permission. There's not much others can do without inviting trouble."

"Yes?" Bertolf von Hanau queried. "What about bankers?"

"Oh, this Fust. He's a mean one."

Everyone muttered agreement.

The next morning when Hans approached the shop,

he sensed something wrong. He couldn't define it. The shop front looked the same. The windowpanes bulged out over the pavement as always. The dark shadows from the interior were no deeper than before. But something had happened.

With caution Hans opened the door. All lay silent within. He went to the inner room and listened. Had he come too early? He could not hear any sound from the workroom. He tried the door. To his surprise, it was unbolted. He stepped inside and surveyed the familiar workshop. He was aware of the smell of damp paper and heavy ink. Piles of printed, dry sheets lay in one corner. Other sheets hung on lines as always.

Why wasn't someone here? Has Herr Fust taken over the shop already? But he couldn't, not until the city court decided.

In a little while the workmen came in, serious and determined. They closed the inner door behind them and set to work.

"You watch in front," Bertolf von Hanau told Hans and Ulrich.

"Watch for what?"

"Just watch, and report if anything happens. And if Peter Schoeffer comes, let me know."

The day passed without incident. At sundown Hans heard a shuffling of feet outside the shop. A group of peasants and townspeople pressed close to the door. "Let us in," a leader called.

Hans ducked behind the counter. If he could crawl back to the inner workshop, he could warn the others. But he had no chance. The townspeople clustered close to the window fronts and cupped their hands over their eyes trying to peer in.

One man butted the door with his shoulder. The heavy door did not budge. Then two men backed off and ran against the door. The heavy thumps made the walls shake.

Bertolf von Hanau ran out from the workshop.

"What is it? What's going on?"

"Those men out there are trying to get in."

Bertolf shook his head. "And they will, too. We'd better get out of here."

"But what can we do?" Heinrich asked. "Where can we go? We'd better face them." He went to the closed door and shouted, "What do you want?"

In reply Hans heard a man call, "Break in the door."

At once the mob stirred and started to push. The heavy door creaked. Hans ran to warn the other workmen, with Bertolf right behind. "What shall we do, men?" Bertolf said. "Give up peacefully and let these fellows take over or give them a run for their money?"

Heinrich, the slow one, bristled like a cock. "No one is going to take over my work."

"What do they want here?" another worker asked. "There's no money in this printing business yet — not until the Bible is done. Do you think Banker Fust is behind all this?"

It was a new thought to Hans, but by this time he would not have been surprised at anything.

"Can't we barricade the door?" someone suggested.

"The press! The press!" Bertolf yelled. "Get behind it. They'd have a time battering it down — unless they used their heads." He called toward the

crowd: "What do you want?"

A peasant waved a tall, lighted taper. "We have come to exorcise the devil."

The crowd of people behind him pushed forward, then fell back, uncertain. Where had they come from? What were they after? In the uneasy moments that followed, Hans had time to remember — first, the neighbors standing fearfully before Herr Mueller's house so long ago, then the peddler, and the old woman. All feared the devil's hand in this new art. All were afraid of new ways.

The crowd muttered among themselves. A quiet, intense undertow pushed Hans back against the door.

"Fire will cleanse, will purge, will wipe out the scourge of devil-begotten ideas," the peasant leader intoned.

Hans jumped up on the counter. "Herr Gutenberg is making the Bible for many people," he shouted. "It will be used in churches. Everyone will benefit from hearing God's Word from the Bible. Herr Gutenberg has had divine inspiration."

At these words, the spokesman thrust his taper high. "God did not say to print His words. They are to be written by hand, just as they have been from the beginning. We shall exorcise the devil. Let us in."

The mass of people shoved forward past Hans and pounded on the door. The door opened. Bertolf and Heinrich stood at the head of the workers. With linked arms they formed a human chain and pushed into the crowd.

With slow, relentless pressure, as heavy as the turn of the press screw itself, the workmen thrust back the mob. Once out on the street, a free-for-all fight broke out.

Hans heard shouts, curses, the thump of falling bodies and groans. He kept out of the way. How long the fight continued, Hans could not determine. But a new sound came to his ears — the sound of ferocious dogs barking at the top of their lungs. Herr Mueller's watchdogs! Hans knew it. Someone must have told him. Then Hans realized he had not seen Ulrich during the fight.

The arrival of the dogs put the townspeople into complete panic. They scattered in all directions. In a little while, only Gutenberg's loyal crew, Herr Mueller, his panting dogs, and a triumphant Ulrich remained.

"Yes, I went to Herr Mueller's," he told Hans.

Herr Mueller appeared pleased. "I only wish Herr Fust had been here, too." He fastened leashes on the dogs and went home. The workmen left too, nursing bruises and cuts, but exulting in the victorious battle. "Nobody will be back tonight," they told each other.

"Go tell the master what happened," Hans suggested to Ulrich. "I'm going to stay here for a while."

The bolts on the door had been shattered, and Hans had no difficulty letting himself into the shop. A stealthy noise outside made him turn and stare into the darkness. He saw two men slipping toward the door. They had not seen him, he knew. He recognized the peasant leader. Was he still determined to exorcise the devil?

Hans crept on hands and knees to the inner workshop. Nothing was clear in his mind as to what he would do. He flung himself under the desk by the window, but realized he would be spotted the instant someone came in with a lighted torch. Perhaps he could squeeze behind the stove, but he dismissed the idea at once.

He heard the men come in. "Destroy everything you see."

"But you will be arrested," the other retorted. "Think a moment. Do nothing you'll be sorry for."

Hans leaned quivering against the press. Where could he go now? How about the press itself? Higher than a man, solid as rock, if he could climb to the top beam. . . . He stood back to look. The top beam was about his own length, and wider than he was. With a last look about the shop, Hans made up his mind. He noted the handholds and footholds. The heavy, almost square foot bar jutting from under the press bed made his first foothold.

Then he stepped on the press bed jutting from the other side, with its two trolley grooves. He stepped up on a thick inner beam, at the same time grasping one of the three jutting slabs, hardly enough for a fingerhold, and bumped his head on the outthrust upper slab. He was stuck. He couldn't move up. The slab was too wide for him to grasp the other edge and pull himself over. He pressed his palms on the top, hoping his hands would stick. He could not climb any further. He had to come around on the printing side and step on the pin which jutted from the side. With one foot on it, he put the other on the top shelf. He nudged the dauber pot to one side, and felt ink on his fingers.

He could not heave himself too high, or he'd hit

the top beams. He stepped out further on the wooden pin. Would it break? He stepped in as close as possible. The upper slab was too thick to get a good grasp with his fingers. Once again he was stuck. He couldn't make it. He would be caught.

The men threw themselves in rhythm against the door. Hans made a frantic jump, clawed and struggled up to the top of the beam. The dust stirred.

The door burst open. A man lit a torch. "Is this the devil's workshop itself?" One of the men dumped the case box over. Hans had a fleeting glimpse of all the letters he would have to sort. But what was he thinking of? The workshop would be gone.

He felt himself about to sneeze. He pressed his forefinger to his upper lip, but it did no good. A sneeze erupted.

Hans resigned himself. All was over now. But the sneeze had a different effect.

"Come away — come away," one of the men implored. "This *is* the devil's own workshop."

The leader agreed. "You're right. This is no place for us. Leave Gutenberg and his works to the devil, and for my money, Peter Schoeffer can go right along with him. Let him do his own mischief."

Peter Schoeffer! Hans lay on the press stunned.

After a long time, Hans climbed down and ran outside. Everyone had gone home. The only signs of the scuffle were a cap here, a torn cloak there.

The next day Gutenberg listened to Hans' report. "I didn't want to believe it. I can face lawsuits, but betrayal? There is no strength left in me to fight. I have done all a man can do. It is up to God, now."

Hans could think of nothing comforting to say.

12
Justice by Law

On November 6, 1455, Johann Gutenberg and Johann Fust met to discuss their grievances before the tribunal in the city hall. Hans and Ulrich sat with Gutenberg's workmen, waiting to be called as witnesses.

The spokesman for the tribunal questioned Herr Fust first. "How much do you want from Herr Gutenberg?"

Head cocked to one side, chin thrust out, Herr Fust did not look at Johann Gutenberg or the workmen. "Two thousand twenty-six florins," he answered.

The spokesman studied the papers he held. "There must be a mistake. These records show that Herr Gutenberg borrowed only eight hundred florins in

1450 and eight hundred in 1452. That makes only sixteen hundred."

Herr Fust bowed. "Your Honor, you have forgotten the amount of interest incurred."

"Very well," the spokesman said. "Now, for what purpose did you lend this money?"

"Herr Gutenberg had a device for metal writing which I thought would prove useful in the future."

"And do you feel that you were mistaken?"

Herr Fust shifted his feet. "No, I was not mistaken, but writing with metal — printing, that is to say — must be done on a businesslike, practical basis. Herr Gutenberg has never been a businessman. If the court please, I would like my money back, with interest." He bowed again and turned to go.

"Please wait, Herr Fust. We have a few more questions. Did you go to Paris in 1453?"

Herr Fust quivered but answered in a firm voice, "Yes."

"For what purpose?"

"To find someone skilled as a scribe and illuminator."

"Did Herr Gutenberg ask you to find someone?"

"No, but I could see he needed someone to help him both as a craftsman and a practical businessman."

"Did you find someone?"

"Yes."

"What is his name?"

"Peter Schoeffer."

"Now, Herr Fust, you must answer truthfully. Is it not true that you and Peter Schoeffer intend to establish a rival printing shop here in Mainz, to share and share alike as partners?"

Herr Fust looked down at his feet and sputtered, "No."

Everyone in the crowded tribunal room gasped. An undertone of indignation spread, then deepened. Hans sprang up, ready to tell what he had seen and overheard, but Ulrich pulled him down.

The spokesman rebuked the spectators. When silence prevailed, he called Peter Schoeffer to stand before him. "What is your name?"

"Peter Schoeffer."

"Are you a citizen of Mainz?"

"No. I come from Gernsheim."

"Did you go to Paris and then return?"

"Yes, in 1454."

"When in Paris, were you a scribe, an illuminator, and manuscript dealer?"

"Yes."

"What work have you been doing for Herr Gutenberg?"

"I was employed as typesetter and proofreader."

"Are you also the foreman of the printing shop?"

"Yes."

"What are your duties?"

"I am in charge of six presses —"

"Presses? Do you mean winepresses?"

"No, no, of course not. Printing presses."

"Is it true, Herr Schoeffer, that you and Herr Gutenberg disagreed on policy?"

"Herr Gutenberg is an artist, not a businessman."

"Answer the question."

"He kept experimenting with smaller and smaller type, saying he wanted to make cheaper and better books, but when I suggested a 48-line Bible instead of 42, he refused."

"On what grounds?"

"That it was not artistic. He also wanted the Bible to look just like handwritten illuminated copies."

"And you didn't approve?"

"Not when he was head over heels in debt."

Hans listened to the questioning. Why didn't the tribunal ask about the copies of the Bible being printed? Why were only Gutenberg's debts discussed?

At recess he heard Herr Fust talking to his legal adviser. "But he did not invent it," Herr Fust was saying. "Printing was well established in Haarlem twenty-five years ago. There is nothing to stop me from opening another printing shop. We can win this suit on the one point alone that Gutenberg did not invent printing with movable type."

Hans sought out Johann Gutenberg and told him what he had heard. "He says you didn't invent printing with movable type," Hans wound up.

"Herr Fust speaks the truth," Gutenberg smiled. "I did not invent this process."

"Then Herr Fust can start his own shop?"

"Of course. You must realize that this printing process was not man-made."

Hans looked at Gutenberg. He was puzzled. "But if it came from God, would He tell several people about it at the same time?"

"It isn't quite like that, Hans. God sends out an urge to fulfill His law. Those who are ready and have prepared themselves to be His instrument will respond. So what difference does it make if a man in Haarlem or all the men in Europe are working on the same idea at the same time? China had movable type before we did."

"Why didn't they give it to us?"

"Because we weren't ready."

Hans thought of the townspeople's fear and misunderstanding of printing. He dimly sensed how the new and strange frightened people.

When Gutenberg was questioned, he replied to the tribunal in a forthright manner.

"Herr Gutenberg, do you claim to be the inventor of movable type?"

"By no means. De Coster of Haarlem worked with movable type as early as 1440."

"When did you complete your presses?"

"In 1450."

"When did you start printing the Bible?"

"In 1450 — the day after I received the first loan from Herr Fust."

"Are we to understand you pledged your printing shop and equipment for the two loans he made?"

"Yes, and he also became my partner."

"Didn't you realize what might happen — that you might not be able to pay back on the designated date?"

"Yes, I realized all was in God's hands."

"Be that as it may, Herr Gutenberg, we are a court of law, and our purpose is to render impartial justice. We wish to know what it is you have invented. Did you invent letter-cutting?"

"No."

"Did you invent the die?"

"No."

"Or how to obtain impressions from the die?"

"No."

"Nor the punches used for stamping letters?"

"No, certainly not."

"Then just what did you do that was new?"

"I have made printing an art. You may examine these pages of the Bible yourself and see whether they are not like the handwriting of the monks. You can also see that each page is perfect. Only that do I lay claim to — that I made printing an art."

The tribunal examined a finished copy of the Bible. Hans could see they were astounded at its perfection.

The tribunal called back Herr Fust. "Now, Herr Fust, what is your complaint?"

"I loaned this man eight hundred gulden in 1450 at six percent interest."

"Did he pay any of this back?"

"No. Not only that, I had to lend him eight hundred gulden more in 1452."

"Why did you do this, knowing Herr Gutenberg had not paid? Is it not true that you wanted to acquire the presses and go into business for yourself?"

"No, no. That is not true. I just wanted my investment back."

A growl of protest rose from Gutenberg's workmen. Hans yearned to testify that he had seen the press being moved and that he had heard Peter Schoeffer say it was for Herr Fust's use. Would he be called as a witness?

The questioning went on.

"You made yourself Herr Gutenberg's partner. Why?"

"Just a matter of business. Five years have passed, and I haven't received a cent. I ask the tribunal to grant me the sum owed."

"Is the Bible finished yet?"

"No. It has to be bound and rubricated."

"Who is doing this?"

"Heinrich Cremer, vicar of St. Stephen's."

"When does he plan to be through?"

"July or August, 1456."

Other witnesses included Bertolf von Hanau and Heinrich Keifer. Both testified that Gutenberg was satisfied with nothing less than perfection.

"Did he waste money?"

"No."

"How do you account for his using so much?"

"There were wages, house rent, parchment, paper, ink, and the master wanted only perfect work."

The tribunal called no other witnesses. The truth lay concealed. Herr Fust, Peter Schoeffer, and Johann Gutenberg's workmen all knew that a rival printing shop had been prepared.

The tribunal rendered its verdict. Johann Gutenberg would have to pay back the money he had borrowed.

Johann Gutenberg could not pay any of it.

Not long afterward, Hans, Ulrich, and the rest of the loyal workmen stood in front of the printing shop and watched Banker Fust's men remove Johann Gutenberg's goods and equipment. Hans picked up an ink dauber dropped by one of Fust's men. The ink stained his fingers. He tried to wipe them clean, but the stains remained, like a promise for the future.

Half-forgotten words of the prior echoed in Hans' mind. "For every gift, God demands a sacrifice," he had said. Then Brother John's words came back to him. "God tests us by opposites."

A thrill of painful understanding ran through Hans.

God had given Johann Gutenberg his greatest test — taking away all he had in worldly goods. Yet God's Word lived now in a new form destined to benefit millions of people still unborn. Hans dimly sensed the wonder of it all.

When Fust's men left, Johann Gutenberg gathered his workmen in the empty printing shop, sank to his knees in prayer, holding his empty hands up to God.

Someone burst through the door. Lorentz, Gutenberg's servant, shouted, "Master, master! We have a patron! Conrad Homery, syndic of Mainz, will pay for everything — new presses, new types — everything! Master, it is the hand of God!" He stopped in embarrassment.

Johann Gutenberg rose with a smile. "Why, yes. I never doubted it."

The workmen cheered, wept, and pounded each other on the back.

Hans held up his ink-stained fingers and grinned at Ulrich. There would be much more ink on their fingers in the days to come.

THE AUTHOR

Following three years of special study in creative writing, **Louise A. Vernon** began her successful series of religious-heritage juveniles. She teaches creative writing in the San Jose, California, public school district.

Mrs. Vernon re-creates for children the stories of Reformation times and acquaints them with great figures in church history. She has traveled throughout England and Germany researching firsthand the settings for her stories. In each book she places a child on the scene with the historical character and involves him in an exciting plot.

The National Association of Christian Schools, representing more then 8,000 Christian educators, honored *Ink on His Fingers* (Gutenberg) as one of the two best children's books with a Christian message released in 1972.

Mrs. Vernon is author of *Peter and the Pilgrims* (early America), *Strangers in the Land* (the Huguenots), *The Secret Church* (the Anabaptists), *The Bible Smuggler* (William Tyndale), *Key to the Prison* (George Fox and the Quakers), *Night Preacher* (Menno Simons and the Anabaptists), *The Beggars' Bible* (John Wycliffe), *Ink on His Fingers* (Johann Gutenberg), *Doctor in Rags* (Paracelsus and the Hutterites), *Thunderstorm in Church* (Martin Luther), *A Heart Strangely Warmed* (John Wesley), and *The Man Who Laid the Egg* (Erasmus).